Java Precisely

Second Edition

Peter Sestoft

Java Precisely

Second Edition

The MIT Press
Cambridge, Massachusetts
London, England

MIT Press books may be purchased at special quantity discounts for business or sales promotional use. For information, please email special_sales@mitpress.mit.edu or write to Special Sales Department, The MIT Press, 55 Hayward Street, Cambridge, MA 02142.

This book was set in Times by the author using LaTeX.

Printed and bound in the United States of America.

Library of Congress Cataloging-in-Publication Data

Sestoft, Peter.
   Java precisely / Peter Sestoft — 2nd ed.
      p.   cm.
   Includes bibliographic references and index.
   ISBN 978-0-262-69325-7(pbk. : alk. paper)
   1. Java (Computer program language)   I. Title.

QA76.73.J38S435 2005
005.13′3—dc22   2005043349

10   9   8   7   6   5   4

Contents

Preface

This second edition of *Java Precisely* gives a concise description of the Java programming language, version 5.0. It is a quick reference for the reader who has already learned (or is learning) Java from a standard textbook and who wants to know the language in more detail. The book presents the entire Java programming language and essential parts of the class libraries: the collection classes and the input-output classes.

General rules are shown on left-hand pages mostly, and corresponding examples are shown on right-hand pages only. All examples are fragments of legal Java programs. The complete ready-to-run example programs are available from the book Web site <http://www.itu.dk/people/sestoft/javaprecisely/>.

This second edition adds material about autoboxing of primitive types (section 5.4), string formatting (section 7.1), variable-arity methods (section 9.9), the enhanced `for` statement (section 12.5.2), enum types (section 14), generic types and methods (section 21), reflection (section 24) and meta-data annotations (section 25), and in general has been updated for the changes from Java 1.4 to Java 5.0. The final section 26 summarizes and illustrates the new features of Java 5.0 and compares them to the C# programming language.

The book does not cover garbage collection, finalization and weak references, details of IEEE754 floating-point numbers, or Javadoc.

Two mistakes were corrected in the second printing of the second edition. Since then, only the book's Web site link above has been changed.

Acknowledgments Thanks to Rasmus Lund, Niels Hallenberg, Hans Henrik Løvengreen, Christian Gram, Jan Clausen, Anders Peter Ravn, Bruce Conrad, Brendan Humphreys, Hans Rischel, Ken Friis Larsen, Dan Becker, Mads Jeppe Tarp-Johansen, Kasper Østerbye, Kasper Bilsted Graversen, Søren Eduard Jacobsen, Paul van Bemmelen, Axel Tobias Schreiner and David Hemmendinger for their useful comments, suggestions, and corrections. Special thanks to Rasmus Lund for letting me adapt his collections diagram for this book, and to Kasper Østerbye for campaigning for a reflection chapter and providing a first draft of it.

It was a pleasure to work with Robert Prior, Valerie Geary, Deborah Cantor-Adams and Krista Magnuson at The MIT Press. Thanks also to the Royal Veterinary and Agricultural University, Denmark and the IT University of Copenhagen, Denmark, for their support.

Notational Conventions

Symbol	Meaning
a	Expression or value of array type
b	Boolean or byte array
C	Class
cs	Character array (type char [])
cseq	Character sequence (type CharSequence)
E	Exception type
e	Expression
f	Field
I	Interface
i	Expression or value of integer type
m	Method
o	Expression or value of object type
p	Package
s	Expression of type String
sig	Signature of method or constructor
t	Type (primitive type or reference type)
T, U, K, V	Type parameter in generic type or method
u	Expression or value of thread type
v	Value of any type
x	Variable or parameter or field or array element

Java Precisely

1 Running Java: Compilation, Loading, and Execution

Before a Java program can be executed, it must be compiled and loaded. The compiler checks that the Java program is *legal:* that the program conforms to the Java syntax or grammar, that operators (such as +) are applied to operands (such as 5 and x) of the correct type, and so on. If so, the compiler generates so-called *class files*. Execution may then be started by loading the needed class files.

Thus running a Java program involves three stages: *compilation* (checks that the program is well-formed), *loading* (loads and initializes classes), and *execution* (runs the program code).

2 Names and Reserved Names

A *legal name* (of a variable, method, field, parameter, class, interface or package) starts with a letter or dollar sign ($) or underscore (_), and continues with zero or more letters or dollar signs or underscores or digits (0–9). Avoid dollar signs in class and interface names. Uppercase letters and lowercase letters are considered distinct. A legal name cannot be one of the following *reserved names:*

```
abstract   char       else       for          interface   protected   switch         try
assert     class      enum       goto         long        public      synchronized   void
boolean    const      extends    if           native      return      this           volatile
break      continue   false      implements   new         short       throw          while
byte       default    final      import       null        static      throws
case       do         finally    instanceof   package     strictfp    transient
catch      double     float      int          private     super       true
```

3 Java Naming Conventions

The following naming conventions are often followed, although not enforced by Java:

- If a name is composed of several words, then each word (except possibly the first one) begins with an uppercase letter. Examples: `setLayout`, `addLayoutComponent`.

- Names of variables, fields, and methods begin with a lowercase letter. Examples: `vehicle`, `myVehicle`.

- Names of classes and interfaces begin with an uppercase letter. Examples: `Cube`, `ColorCube`.

- Named constants (such as `final static` fields) are written entirely in uppercase, and the parts of composite names are separated by underscores (_). Examples: `CENTER`, `MAX_VALUE`.

- Package names are sequences of dot-separated lowercase names. Example: `java.awt.event`. For uniqueness, they are often prefixed with reverse domain names, as in `com.sun.xml.util`.

4 Comments and Program Layout

Comments have no effect on the execution of the program but may be inserted anywhere to help humans understand the program. There are two forms: one-line comments and delimited comments.

Program layout has no effect on the computer's execution of the program but is used to help humans understand the structure of the program.

Example 1 Comments

```
class Comment {
  // This is a one-line comment; it extends to the end of the line.
  /* This is a delimited comment,
     extending over several lines.
  */
  int /* This delimited comment extends over part of a line */ x = 117;
}
```

Example 2 Recommended Program Layout Style
For reasons of space this layout style is not always followed in this book.

```
class Layout {                        // Class declaration
  int x;

  Layout(int x) {
    this.x = x;                       // One-line body
  }

  int sum(int y) {                    // Multi-line body
    if (x > 0) {                      // If statement
      return x + y;                   // Single statement
    } else if (x < 0) {               // Nested if-else, block statement
      int res = -x + y;
      return res * 117;
    } else { // x == 0                // Terminal else, block statement
      int sum = 0;
      for (int i=0; i<10; i++) {      // For loop
        sum += (y - i) * (y - i);
      }
      return sum;
    }
  }

  static boolean checkdate(int mth, int day) {
    int length;
    switch (mth) {                    // Switch statement
    case 2:                           // Single case
      length = 28; break;
    case 4: case 6: case 9: case 11:  // Multiple case
      length = 30; break;
    case 1: case 3: case 5: case 7: case 8: case 10: case 12:
      length = 31; break;
    default:
      return false;
    }
    return (day >= 1) && (day <= length);
  }
}
```

5 Types

A *type* is a set of values and operations on them. A type is either a primitive type or a reference type.

5.1 Primitive Types

A *primitive type* is either boolean or one of the *numeric types* char, byte, short, int, long, float, and double. The primitive types, example literals (that is, constants), size in bits (where 8 bits equals 1 byte), and value range, are shown in the table opposite.

The integer types are exact within their range. They use signed 2's complement representation (except for char), so when the most positive number in a type is *max*, then the most negative number is $-max - 1$. The floating-point types are inexact and follow IEEE754, with the number of significant digits indicated by "sigdig." For character escape sequences such as \u0000, see page 10.

5.2 Reference Types

A *reference type* is either a class type defined by a class declaration (section 9.1), or an interface type defined by an interface declaration (section 13.1), or an array type (section 5.3), or an enum type (section 14).

A value of reference type is either null or a reference to an object or array. The special value null denotes "no object." The literal null, denoting the null value, can have any reference type.

5.3 Array Types

An *array type* has the form t[], where t is any type. An array type t[] is a reference type. Hence a value of array type t[] is either null, or is a reference to an array whose element type is precisely t (when t is a primitive type), or is a subtype of t (when t is a reference type).

5.4 Boxing: Wrapping Primitive Types As Reference Types

For every primitive type there is a corresponding wrapper class, which is a reference type. The wrapper classes are listed in the table opposite. An object of a wrapper class contains a single value of the corresponding primitive type.

A wrapper class must be used when a value of primitive type is passed to a method that expects a reference type, or stored in a variable or field of reference type. For instance, to store an int in a collection (section 22) one must wrap it as an Integer object.

The conversion from primitive type to wrapper class is called *boxing*, and the opposite conversion is called *unboxing*. Boxing and unboxing are performed automatically (in Java 5.0) when needed. Boxing and unboxing may also be performed explicitly using operations such as new Integer(i) to box the integer i, and o.intValue() or (int)o to unbox the Integer object o. If o is null, then unboxing of o will fail at run-time by throwing NullPointerException. Because of automatic unboxing, a Boolean value may be used in conditional statements (if, for, while and do-while) and in logical operators (such as !, &&, ?: and so on); and Integer and other integer type wrapper classes may be used in switch statements.

A boxed value can be unboxed only to a value of the boxed type, or to a supertype. Thus an Integer object can be unboxed to an int or a long because long is a supertype of int, but not to a char or byte or short.

The wrapper classes Byte, Short, Integer, Long, Float, and Double have the common superclass Number.

Primitive Types

Type	Kind	Example Literals	Size	Range	Wrapper
`boolean`	logical	`false`, `true`	1		Boolean
`char`	integer	`' '`, `'0'`, `'A'`, ...	16	`\u0000` ... `\uFFFF` (unsigned)	Character
`byte`	integer	`0, 1, -1, 117,` ...	8	$max = 127$	Byte
`short`	integer	`0, 1, -1, 117,` ...	16	$max = 32767$	Short
`int`	integer	`0, 1, -1, 117,` ...	32	$max = 2147483647$	Integer
`long`	integer	`0L, 1L, -1L, 117L,` ...	64	$max = 9223372036854775807$	Long
`float`	floating-pt	`-1.0f, 0.49f, 3E8f,` ...	32	$\pm 10^{-38} \ldots \pm 10^{38}$, sigdig 6–7	Float
`double`	floating-pt	`-1.0, 0.49, 3E8,` ...	64	$\pm 10^{-308} \ldots \pm 10^{308}$, sigdig 15–16	Double

Integer Literals

Integer literals (of type `byte`, `char`, `short`, `int`, or `long`) may be written in three different bases.

Notation	Base	Distinction	Example Integer Literals
Decimal	10	No leading 0	`1234567890, 127, -127`
Octal	8	Leading 0	`01234567, 0177, -0177`
Hexadecimal	16	Leading 0x	`0xABCDEF0123, 0x7F, -0x7F`

Example 3 Automatic Boxing and Unboxing

```
Boolean bb1 = false, bb2 = !bb1;    // Boxing to [false] [true]
Integer bi1 = 117;                  // Boxing to [117]
Double bd1 = 1.2;                   // Boxing to [1.2]
boolean b1 = bb1;                   // Unboxing, result false
if (bb1)                            // Unboxing, result false
  System.out.println("Not true");
int i1 = bi1 + 2;                   // Unboxing, result 119
// short s = bi1;                   // Illegal
long l = bi1;                       // Legal: int is subtype of long
Integer bi2 = bi1 + 2;             // Unboxing, boxing, result [119]
Integer[] biarr = { 2, 3, 5, 7, 11 };
int sum = 0;
for (Integer bi : biarr)
  sum += bi;                        // Unboxing in loop body
for (int i : biarr)                 // Unboxing in loop header
  sum += i;
int i = 1934;
Integer bi4 = i, bi5 = i;
// Prints true true true false; bi4==bi5 is a reference comparison:
System.out.format("%b %b %b %b%n", i==i, bi4==i, i==bi5, bi4==bi5);
Boolean bbn = null;
boolean b = bbn;                    // Compiles OK, fails at run-time
if (bbn)                            // Compiles OK, fails at run-time
  System.out.println("Not true");
Integer bin = null;
Integer bi6 = bin + 2;             // Compiles OK, fails at run-time
```

5.5 Subtypes and Compatibility

A type t1 may be a *subtype* of a type t2, in which case t2 is a *supertype* of t1. Intuitively this means that any value v1 of type t1 can be used where a value of type t2 is expected. When t1 and t2 are reference types, t1 must provide at least the functionality (methods and fields) provided by t2. In particular, any value v1 of type t1 may be bound to a variable or field or parameter x2 of type t2, e.g., by the assignment x2 = v1 or by parameter passing. We also say that types t1 and t2 are *compatible*. The following rules determine when a type t1 is a subtype of a type t2:

- Every type is a subtype of itself.
- If t1 is a subtype of t2, and t2 is a subtype of t3, then t1 is a subtype of t3.
- If t1 and t2 are primitive types, and there is a widening (W or L) conversion from t1 to t2 according to the table opposite, then t1 is a subtype of t2.
- If t1 and t2 are classes, then t1 is a subtype of t2 if t1 is a subclass of t2.
- If t1 and t2 are interfaces, then t1 is a subtype of t2 if t1 is a subinterface of t2.
- If t1 is a class and t2 is an interface, then t1 is a subtype of t2 provided that t1 (is a subclass of a class that) implements t2 or implements a subinterface of t2.
- Array type t1[] is a subtype of array type t2[] if reference type t1 is a subtype of reference type t2.
- Any reference type t, including any array type, is also a subtype of predefined class Object.

No primitive type is a subtype of a reference type and no reference type is a subtype of a primitive type. But there are automatic boxing and unboxing conversions between a primitive type and its wrapper class; see section 5.4.

5.6 Signatures and Subsumption

A *signature* has form $m(t_1, \ldots, t_n)$, where m is a method or constructor name, and $(t_1, \ldots, t_n)$ is a list of non-generic types; see example 33.

We say that a signature $sig_1 = m(t_1, \ldots, t_n)$ *subsumes* signature $sig_2 = m(u_1, \ldots, u_n)$ if each u_i is a subtype of t_i. We also say that sig_2 is *more specific* than sig_1. Note that the method name m and the number *n* of types must be the same in the two signatures. Since every type t_i is a subtype of itself, every signature subsumes itself. In a collection of signatures there may be one that is subsumed by all others; such a signature is called the *most specific* signature.

5.7 Type Conversion

A *type conversion* converts a value from one type to another. A *widening* conversion converts from a type to a supertype (or the type itself). A *narrowing* conversion converts from a type to another type. A narrowing conversion requires an explicit *type cast*, see section 11.11, except in an assignment x = e or initialization where e is a compile-time integer constant; see section 11.5.

The legal type conversions between primitive types are shown in the table opposite. The primitive type boolean cannot be converted to any other primitive type. A type cast between primitive types never fails at run-time.

Conversion between Primitive Types

The letter C marks a narrowing conversion that requires a type cast (t)e, see section 11.11; W marks a widening conversion that preserves the value; and L marks a widening conversion that may cause a loss of precision. A narrowing integer conversion discards those (most significant) bits that cannot be represented in the smaller integer type. Conversion from an integer type to a floating-point type (float or double) produces a floating-point approximation of the integer value. Conversion from a floating-point type to an integer type discards the fractional part of the number; that is, it rounds toward zero. When converting a too-large floating-point number to a long or int, the result is the best approximation (that is, the type's largest positive or the largest negative representable number); conversion to byte or short or char is done by converting to int and then to the requested type.

From Type	To Type						
	char	byte	short	int	long	float	double
char	W	C	C	W	W	W	W
byte	C	W	W	W	W	W	W
short	C	C	W	W	W	W	W
int	C	C	C	W	W	L	W
long	C	C	C	C	W	L	L
float	C	C	C	C	C	W	W
double	C	C	C	C	C	C	W

Example 4 Conversion between Primitive Types

This example shows lossy (L) and lossless (W) widening conversions to float and double as well as narrowing conversions (C) from int and double. Example 48 shows primitive conversions in assignments.

```
private static void floatdouble(float f, double d)
{ System.out.println(f + " " + d); }
private static void bytecharshort(byte b, char c, short s)
{ System.out.println(b + " " + (int)c + " " + s); }
private static void intint(int i1, int i2)
{ System.out.println(i1 + " " + i2); }
...
int i1 = 1000111222, i2 = 40000, i3 = -1;
floatdouble(i1, i1);                          // L W: 1.00011123E9 1.000111222E9
bytecharshort((byte)i2, (char)i2, (short)i2); // C C C: 64 40000 -25536
bytecharshort((byte)i3, (char)i3, (short)i3); // C C C: -1 65535 -1
intint((int)1.9, (int)-1.9);                  // C C: 1 -1
intint((int)1.5, (int)-1.5);                  // C C: 1 -1
intint((int)2.5, (int)-2.5);                  // C C: 2 -2
```

Example 5 Method Signature Subsumption

- m(double,double) subsumes itself and m(double,int) and m(int,double) and m(int,int).
- m(double,int) subsumes itself and m(int,int).
- m(int,double) subsumes itself and m(int,int).
- m(double,int) does not subsume m(int,double), nor the other way round.
- The collection m(double,int), m(int,int) has the most specific signature m(int,int).
- The collection m(double,int), m(int,double) has no most specific signature.

6   Variables, Parameters, Fields, and Scope

A *variable* is declared inside a method, constructor, initializer block, or block statement (section 12.2). The variable can be used only in that block statement (or method or constructor or initializer block), and only after its declaration.

A *parameter* is a special kind of variable: it is declared in the parameter list of a method or constructor, and is given a value when the method or constructor is called. The parameter can be used only in that method or constructor.

A *field* is declared inside a class, but not inside a method or constructor or initializer block of the class. It can be used anywhere in the class, also textually before its declaration.

6.1   Values Bound to Variables, Parameters, or Fields

A variable, parameter, or field of primitive type holds a *value* of that type, such as the boolean `false`, the integer `117`, or the floating-point number `1.7`. A variable, parameter, or field of reference type t either has the special value `null` or holds a reference to an object or array. If it is an object, then the run-time class of that object must be t or a subclass of t.

6.2   Variable Declarations

The purpose of a variable is to hold a value during the execution of a block statement (or method or constructor or initializer block). A *variable-declaration* has one of the forms

> *variable-modifier type varname1, varname2, ... ;*
> *variable-modifier type varname1 = initializer1, ... ;*

A *variable-modifier* may be `final` or absent. If a variable is declared `final`, then it must be initialized or assigned at most once at run-time (exactly once if it is ever used): it is a *named constant*. However, if the variable has reference type, then the object or array pointed to by the variable may still be modified. A *variable initializer* may be an expression or an array initializer (section 8.2).

Execution of the variable declaration will reserve space for the variable, then evaluate the initializer, if any, and store the resulting value in the variable. Unlike a field, a variable is not given a default value when declared, but the compiler checks that it has been given a value before it is used.

6.3   Scope of Variables, Parameters, and Fields

The *scope* of a name is that part of the program in which the name is visible. The scope of a variable extends from just after its declaration to the end of the innermost enclosing block statement. The scope of a method or constructor parameter is the entire method or constructor body. For a control variable x declared in a `for` statement

> `for (int x = ...; ...; ...)` *body*

the scope is the entire `for` statement, including the header and the body.

Within the scope of a variable or parameter x, one cannot redeclare x. However, one may declare a variable x within the scope of a field x, thus *shadowing* the field. Hence the scope of a field x is the entire class, except where shadowed by a variable or parameter of the same name, and except for initializers preceding the field's declaration (section 9.1).

Example 6 Variable Declarations

```
public static void main(String[] args) {
  int a, b, c;
  int x = 1, y = 2, z = 3;
  int ratio = z/x;
  final double PI = 3.141592653589;
  boolean found = false;
  final int maxyz;
  if (z > y) maxyz = z; else maxyz = y;
}
```

Example 7 Scope of Fields, Parameters, and Variables

This program declares five variables or fields, all called x, and shows where each one is in scope (visible). The variables and fields are labeled #1, ..., #5 for reference.

```
class Scope {
  ...                   //
  void m1(int x) {      // Declaration of parameter x (#1)
    ...                 // x #1 in scope
  }                     //
  ...                   //
  void m2(int v2) {     //
    ...                 // x #5 in scope
  }                     //
  ...                   //
  void m3(int v3) {     //
    ...                 // x #5 in scope
    int x;              // Declaration of variable x (#2)
    ...                 // x #2 in scope
  }                     //
  ...                   //
  void m4(int v4) {     //
    ...                 // x #5 in scope
    {                   //
      int x;            // Declaration of variable x (#3)
      ...               // x #3 in scope
    }                   //
    ...                 // x #5 in scope
    {                   //
      int x;            // Declaration of variable x (#4)
      ...               // x #4 in scope
    }                   //
    ...                 // x #5 in scope
  }                     //
  ...                   //
  int x;                // Declaration of field x (#5)
  ...                   // x #5 in scope
}
```

7   Strings

A *string* is an object of the predefined class String. It is immutable: once created it cannot be changed. A string literal is a sequence of characters within double quotes: "New York", "A38", "", and so on. Internally, a character is stored as a number using the Unicode character encoding, whose character codes 0–127 coincide with the old ASCII character encoding. String literals and character literals may use character *escape sequences*:

Escape Code	Meaning
\b	backspace
\t	horizontal tab
\n	newline
\f	form feed (page break)
\r	carriage return
\"	the double quote character
\'	the single quote character
\\	the backslash character
ddd	the character whose character code is the three-digit octal number *ddd*
\u*dddd*	the character whose character code is the four-digit hexadecimal number *dddd*

A character escape sequence represents a single character. Since the letter A has code 65 (decimal), which is written 101 in octal and 0041 in hexadecimal, the string literal "A\101\u0041" is the same as "AAA". If s1 and s2 are expressions of type String and v is an expression of any type, then

- s1.length() of type int is the length of s1, that is, the number of characters in s1.
- s1.equals(s2) of type boolean is true if s1 and s2 contain the same sequence of characters, and false otherwise; equalsIgnoreCase is similar but does not distinguish lowercase and uppercase.
- s1.charAt(i) of type char is the character at position i in s1, counting from 0. If the index i is less than 0, or greater than or equal to s1.length(), then StringIndexOutOfBoundsException is thrown.
- s1.toString() of type String is the same object as s1.
- String.valueOf(v) returns the string representation of v, which can have any primitive type (section 5.1) or reference type. When v has reference type and is not null, then it is converted using v.toString(); if it is null, then it is converted to the string "null". Any class C inherits from Object a default toString method that produces strings of the form C@2a5734, where 2a5734 is some memory address, but toString may be overridden to produce more useful strings.
- s1 + s2 has the same meaning as s1.concat(s2): it constructs the concatenation of s1 and s2, a new String consisting of the characters of s1 followed by the characters of s2. Both s1 + v and v + s1 are evaluated by converting v to a string with String.valueOf(v), thus using v.toString() when v has reference type, and then concatenating the resulting strings.
- s1.compareTo(s2) returns a negative integer, zero, or a positive integer, according as s1 precedes, equals, or follows s2 in the usual lexicographical ordering based on the Unicode character encoding. If s1 or s2 is null, then the exception NullPointerException is thrown. Method compareToIgnoreCase is similar but does not distinguish lowercase and uppercase.
- s1.substring(int i, int j) returns a new String of the characters from s1 with indexes i..(j-1). Throws IndexOutOfBoundsException if i<0 or i>j or j>s1.length.
- s1.subSequence(int i, int j) is like substring but returns a CharSequence (section 23.7).
- More String methods are described in the Java class library documentation [3].

Example 8 Equality of Strings, and the Subtlety of the (+) Operator

```
String s1 = "abc";
String s2 = s1 + "";        // New object, but contains same text as s1
String s3 = s1;             // Same object as s1
String s4 = s1.toString();  // Same object as s1
// The following statements print false, true, true, true, true:
System.out.println("s1 and s2 identical objects: " + (s1 == s2));
System.out.println("s1 and s3 identical objects: " + (s1 == s3));
System.out.println("s1 and s4 identical objects: " + (s1 == s4));
System.out.println("s1 and s2 contain same text: " + (s1.equals(s2)));
System.out.println("s1 and s3 contain same text: " + (s1.equals(s3)));
// These two statements print 35A and A1025 because (+) is left-associative:
System.out.println(10 + 25 + "A");  // Same as (10 + 25) + "A"
System.out.println("A" + 10 + 25);  // Same as ("A" + 10) + 25
```

Example 9 Concatenating All Command Line Arguments

When concatenating many strings, use a string builder instead (chapter 20 and example 100).

```
public static void main(String[] args) {
  String res = "";
  for (int i=0; i<args.length; i++)
    res += args[i];
  System.out.println(res);
}
```

Example 10 Counting the Number of e's in a String

```
static int ecount(String s) {
  int ecount = 0;
  for (int i=0; i<s.length(); i++)
    if (s.charAt(i) == 'e')
      ecount++;
  return ecount;
}
```

Example 11 Determining Whether Strings Occur in Lexicographically Increasing Order

```
static boolean sorted(String[] a) {
  for (int i=1; i<a.length; i++)
    if (a[i-1].compareTo(a[i]) > 0)
      return false;
  return true;
}
```

Example 12 Using a Class That Declares a `toString` Method

The class Point (example 24) declares a `toString` method that returns a string of the point coordinates. The operator (+) calls the `toString` method implicitly to format the Point objects.

```
Point p1 = new Point(10, 20), Point p2 = new Point(30, 40);
System.out.println("p1 is " + p1);       // Prints: p1 is (10, 20)
System.out.println("p2 is " + p2);       // Prints: p2 is (30, 40)
p2.move(7, 7);
System.out.println("p2 is " + p2);       // Prints: p2 is (37, 47)
```

7.1 String Formatting (Java 5.0)

Formatting of numbers, characters, dates, times, and other data may be done using a formatting string `fmt` containing *formatting specifiers*, using one of these methods:

- `String.format(fmt, v1, ..., vn)` returns a String produced from `fmt` by replacing formatting specifiers with the strings resulting from formatting the values `v1, ..., vn`.

- `strm.format(fmt, v1, ..., vn)`, where `strm` is a PrintWriter or PrintStream (section 23.6), constructs a string as above, outputs it to `strm`, and returns `strm`.

- `strm.printf(fmt, v1, ..., vn)` behaves exactly as `strm.format(fmt, v1, ..., vn)`.

These methods exist also in a version that take a Locale object as first argument; see examples 16 and 17. Formatting specifiers are described in sections 7.1.1 and 7.1.2 below. If a value `vi` is of the wrong type for a given formatting specifier, or if the formatting specifier is ill-formed, then a call to the above methods will throw an exception of class IllegalFormatException or one of its subclasses.

7.1.1 Formatting of Numeric, Character, and General Types

A formatting specifier for numeric, character, and general types has this form:

%[*index*$] [*flags*] [*width*] [.*precision*] *conversion*

The *index* is an integer $1, 2, \ldots$ indicating the value v_{index} to format; the *conversion* indicates what operation is used to format the value; the *width* indicates the minimum number of characters used to format the value; the *flags* indicate how that width should be used (where "-" means left-justification, or padding on the right, and "0" means padding with zero); and *precision* limits the output, such as the number of fractional digits. Each of the four parts in brackets [ ] is optional; the only mandatory parts are the percent sign (%) and the *conversion*.

The documentation for Java API class java.util.Formatter gives the full details of number formatting. The table below shows the legal *conversions* on numbers (I = integers, F = floating-point numbers, IF = both), characters (C) and general types (G). An uppercase conversion such as X produces uppercase output.

Format	conversion	flags	precision	Type
Decimal	d	-+ 0,(		I
Octal	o	-#0		I
Hexadecimal	x or X	-#0		I
Hexadecimal significand and exponent	a or A	-#+ 0		F
General: scientific or fractional	g or G	-#+ 0,(	Max. significant digits	IF
Fixed-point number	f	-#+ 0,(	Fractional digits	IF
Scientific notation	e or E	-#+ 0,(	Fractional digits	IF
Unicode character	c or C	-		C
Boolean: "true" or "false"	b or B	-		Boolean
Hexadecimal hashcode of value, or "null"	h or H	-		G
Determined by value's formatTo method	s or S	-		G
A percent symbol (%)	%	(none)		
Platform-specific newline	n	(none)		

Example 13 Aligning Strings Using the `String.format` Method
The code `%` begins each of the three formatting specifiers, `1$` refers to the first value (`"Oslo"`), conversion `s` means string formatting, width 7 means seven characters minimum width, and "-" means left-justification. The result `res` is `|Oslo|␣␣␣Oslo|Oslo␣␣␣|`, where the symbol `␣` denotes a blank (space).

```
String res = String.format("|%1$s|%1$7s|%1$-7s|", "Oslo");
```

Example 14 Aligning Numbers in Columns Using the `out.format` Method
Three lines each with five numbers in the range 0–999 are printed, with the numbers right-justified in a field 4 characters wide so that they form five columns. The formatting specifier `%4d` uses implicit indexing; one might equivalently use explicit indexing `#1$4d` for the same effect. Note the use of `%n` to denote a newline.

```
Random rnd = new Random();                          // Random number generator
for (int i=0; i<3; i++) {
  for (int j=0; j<5; j++)
    System.out.format("%4d", rnd.nextInt(1000));    // Random integer 0..999
  System.out.format("%n");                          // Newline
}
```

Some Integer Formatting Specifiers and Their Effect

Number							
	`%d<`	`%+d<`	`%8d<`	`%-8d<`	`%08d`	`%,d`	`%(d`
0	`0<`	`+0<`	`       0<`	`0       <`	`00000000`	`0`	`0`
255	`255<`	`+255<`	`     255<`	`255     <`	`00000255`	`255`	`255`
-255	`-255<`	`-255<`	`    -255<`	`-255    <`	`-0000255`	`-255`	`(255)`
1250662	`1250662<`	`+1250662<`	`1250662<`	`1250662 <`	`01250662`	`1,250,662`	`1250662`

Number	Formatting Specifier					
	`%+-,11d<`	`%x`	`%#x`	`%X`	`%o`	`%#o`
0	`+0        <`	`0`	`0x0`	`0`	`0`	`00`
255	`+255      <`	`ff`	`0xff`	`FF`	`377`	`0377`
-255	`-255      <`	`ffffff01`	`0xffffff01`	`FFFFFF01`	`37777777401`	`037777777401`
1250662	`+1,250,662 <`	`131566`	`0x131566`	`131566`	`4612546`	`04612546`

Some Floating-Point Number Formatting Specifiers and Their Effect

Number	Formatting Specifier						
	`%f`	`%.2f`	`%7.2f`	`%07.2f`	`%7.0f`	`%.4g`	`%.4e`
0.0	`0.000000`	`0.00`	`   0.00`	`0000.00`	`     0.`	`0.0000`	`0.0000e+00`
0.1	`0.100000`	`0.10`	`   0.10`	`0000.10`	`     0.`	`0.1000`	`1.0000e-01`
1.0	`1.000000`	`1.00`	`   1.00`	`0001.00`	`     1`	`1.0000`	`1.0000e+00`
1.5	`1.500000`	`1.50`	`   1.50`	`0001.50`	`     2.`	`1.5000`	`1.5000e+00`
-1.5	`-1.500000`	`-1.50`	`  -1.50`	`-001.50`	`    -2.`	`-1.5000`	`-1.5000e+00`
330.8	`330.800000`	`330.80`	` 330.80`	`0330.80`	`   331.`	`330.8000`	`3.3080e+02`
1234.516	`1234.516000`	`1234.52`	`1234.52`	`1234.52`	`  1235.`	`1234.5160`	`1.2345e+03`

7.1.2 Formatting of Dates and Times

A formatting specifier for dates and times has this form:

%[*index*$] [*flag*] [*width*] *conversion*

The *index* and *width* are as in section 7.1.1. The only possible *flag* is "-" which causes left-justification (padding on the right) in connection with a *width* specification. The legal *conversions* are shown below.

Format	*conversion*	Example Result
Hour of the day, 24-hour clock, two digits	tH	21
Hour of the day, 12-hour clock, two digits	tI	09
Hour of the day, 24-hour clock, one or two digits	tk	21
Hour of the day, 12-hour clock, one or two digits	tl	9
Minute within the hour, two digits	tM	06
Seconds within the minute, two digits	tS	07
Milliseconds within the second, three digits	tL	870
Nanosecond within the second, nine digits	tN	870000000
Locale-specific morning/afternoon, lowercase	tp	pm
Locale-specific morning/afternoon, uppercase	tP	PM
Numeric time zone offset from UTC (plus is East)	tz	+0100
Alphabetic time zone abbreviation	tZ	CET
Seconds since the epoch (1970-01-01 00:00:00 UTC)	ts	1078517167
Milliseconds since the epoch	tQ	1078517167870
Locale-specific full month name	tB	March
Locale-specific short month name	tb	Mar
Locale-specific full weekday name	tA	Friday
Locale-specific short weekday name	ta	Fri
Century (year divided by 100)	tC	20
Year, four digits	tY	2004
Year, last two digits	ty	04
Day of year, three digits	tj	065
Month number, two digits	tm	03
Day of month, two digits	td	05
Day of month, one or two digits	te	5
Time of day (hour and minute)	tR	21:06
Time of day (hour, minute, seconds)	tT	21:06:07
Time of day (12-hour clock, minute, seconds)	tr	09:06:07 PM
US-style date (month/day/year)	tD	03/05/04
ISO8601 date (year-month-day)	tF	2004-03-05
Date, time and timezone; similar to POSIX asctime	tc	Fri Mar 05 21:06:07 CET 2004

Example 15 Formatting Dates and Times As Strings

This example prints `2004-09-14 12:09`; months are numbered from 0 in Java's GregorianCalendar class.

```
GregorianCalendar date = new GregorianCalendar(2004, 8, 14, 12, 9, 28);
System.out.format("%1$tF %1$tR%n", date);
```

Example 16 Locale-Specific Formatting of Dates and Times

The formatting of date and time often depends on the locale: language and nationality. For instance, this is the case for the formatting specifier `%tc`. The Locale class is in package `java.util`.

```
Date now = new Date();
System.out.format("%tc%n", now);                     // default locale
System.out.format(Locale.US, "%tc%n", now);          // en_US locale
System.out.format(Locale.GERMANY, "%tc%n", now);     // de_DE locale
```

Example 17 Locale-Specific Formatting of Numbers

Number formatting is locale sensitive: different languages use different decimal separators (point or comma). For instance, this example outputs `1,234,567.90` and `1.234.567,90` and `1 234 567,90` where the spaces in the latter number are special non-breaking spaces (ISO Latin1 character `'\240'`).

```
double d = 1234567.9;
System.out.format(Locale.US,       "%,.2f%n", d);    // en_US locale
System.out.format(Locale.GERMANY,  "%,.2f%n", d);    // de_DE locale
System.out.format(Locale.FRANCE,   "%,.2f%n", d);    // fr_FR locale
```

Some Date and Time Formatting Specifiers and Their Effect

Different languages and countries have very different conventions for writing dates, requiring different formatting specifiers for use with `String.format`. In general, the locale mechanism is not sufficient to write locale-specific dates, except when using the `%tc` formatting specifier. To avoid misunderstandings, do give all four digits of the year, and avoid formats such as `03/05/04` that may have different US and UK interpretations.

Formatting Specifier	Result	Locale	Usage
`%tc`	Fri Mar 05 21:06:07 CET 2004	en_US	US
`%tc`	Fr Mrz 05 21:06:07 CET 2004	de_DE	Germany
`%tc`	ven. mars 05 21:06:07 CET 2004	fr_FR	France
`%1$tD`	03/05/04	en_US	US
`%1$tm/%1$td/%1$ty`	03/05/04	en_US	US
`%1$tm/%1$td/%1$ty %1$tI:%1$tM %1$tP`	03/05/04 09:06 PM	en_US	US
`%1$td.%1$tm.%1$tY %1$tH:%1$tM`	05.03.2004 21:06	en_US	Germany
`%1$td/%1$tm/%1$tY`	05/03/2004	en_US	UK
`%1$td-%1$tb-%1$ty`	05-Mar-04	en_US	US/UK
`%1$tB %1$te, %1$tY`	March 5, 2004	en_US	US
`%1$tA %1$tB %1$te, %1$tY`	Friday March 5, 2004	en_US	US
`%1$tA, %1$te %1$tB %1$tY`	Friday, 5 March 2004	en_US	UK
`%1$te. %1$tB %1$tY`	5. März 2004	de_DE	Germany
`%1$tA %1$te. %1$tB %1$tY`	Freitag 5. März 2004	de_DE	Germany
`%1$tFT%1$tT`	2004-03-05T21:06:07	en_US	RFC3339

8   Arrays

An *array* is an indexed collection of variables, called *elements*. An array has a given *length* $\ell \geq 0$ and a given *element type* t. The elements are indexed by the integers $0, 1, \ldots, \ell - 1$. The value of an expression of array type u[] is either null or a reference to an array whose element type t is a subtype of u. If u is a primitive type, then t must equal u.

8.1   Array Creation and Access

A new array of length ℓ with element type t is created (allocated) using an *array creation expression*:

    new t[ℓ]

where ℓ is an expression of type int. If type t is a primitive type, all elements of the new array are initialized to 0 (when t is byte, char, short, int, or long) or 0.0 (when t is float or double) or false (when t is boolean). If t is a reference type, all elements are initialized to null.

If ℓ is negative, then the exception NegativeArraySizeException is thrown.

Let a be a reference of array type u[], to an array with length ℓ and element type t. Then

- a.length of type int is the length ℓ of a, that is, the number of elements in a.

- The *array access* expression a[i] denotes element number i of a, counting from 0; this expression has type u. The integer expression i is called the *array index*. If the value of i is less than 0 or greater than or equal to a.length, then exception ArrayIndexOutOfBoundsException is thrown.

- When t is a reference type, every array element assignment a[i] = e checks that the value of e is null or a reference to an object whose class C is a subtype of the element type t. If this is not the case, then the exception ArrayStoreException is thrown. This check is made before every array element assignment at run-time, but only for reference types.

8.2   Array Initializers

A variable or field of array type may be initialized at declaration, using an existing array or an *array initializer* for the initial value. An array initializer is a comma-separated list of zero or more expressions enclosed in braces { ... }:

    t[] x = { expression, ..., expression }

The type of each *expression* must be a subtype of t. Evaluation of the initializer causes a distinct new array, whose length equals the number of expressions, to be allocated. Then the expressions are evaluated from left to right and their values are stored in the array, and finally the array is bound to x. Hence x cannot occur in the *expressions:* it has not yet been initialized when they are evaluated.

Array initializers may also be used in connection with array creation expressions:

    new t[] { expression, ..., expression }

Multidimensional arrays can have nested initializers (example 22). Note that there are no array constants: a new distinct array is created every time an array initializer is evaluated.

Example 18 Creating and Using One-Dimensional Arrays
The first half of this example rolls a die 1000 times, then prints the frequencies of the outcomes. The second half creates and initializes an array of String objects.

```
int[] freq = new int[6];                      // All initialized to 0
for (int i=0; i<1000; i++) {                   // Roll dice, count frequencies
  int die = (int)(1 + 6 * Math.random());
  freq[die-1] += 1;
}
for (int c=1; c<=6; c++)
  System.out.println(c + " came up " + freq[c-1] + " times");

String[] number = new String[20];              // Create array of null elements
for (int i=0; i<number.length; i++)            // Fill with strings "A0", ..., "A19"
  number[i] = "A" + i;
for (int i=0; i<number.length; i++)            // Print strings
  System.out.println(number[i]);
```

Example 19 Array Element Assignment Type Check at Run-Time
This program compiles, but at run-time a[2]=d throws ArrayStoreException, since the class of the object bound to d (that is, Double) is not a subtype of a's element type (that is, Integer).

```
Number[] a = new Integer[10];      // Length 10, element type Integer
Double d = new Double(3.14);       // Type Double,  class Double
Integer i = new Integer(117);      // Type Integer, class Integer
Number n = i;                      // Type Number,  class Integer
a[0] = i;                          // OK, Integer is subtype of Integer
a[1] = n;                          // OK, Integer is subtype of Integer
a[2] = d;                          // No, Double not subtype of Integer
```

Example 20 Using an Initialized Array
Method checkdate here behaves the same as checkdate in example 2. The array should be declared outside the method, as shown, otherwise a distinct new array is created for every call to the method.

```
static int[] days = { 31, 28, 31, 30, 31, 30, 31, 31, 30, 31, 30, 31 };
static boolean checkdate(int mth, int day)
{ return (mth >= 1) && (mth <= 12) && (day >= 1) && (day <= days[mth-1]); }
```

Example 21 Creating a String from a Character Array
When replacing character c1 by character c2 in a string, the result can be built in a character array because its length is known. This is 50 percent faster than example 101 which uses a string builder.

```
static String replaceCharChar(String s, char c1, char c2) {
  char[] res = new char[s.length()];
  for (int i=0; i<s.length(); i++)
    if (s.charAt(i) == c1)
      res[i] = c2;
    else
      res[i] = s.charAt(i);
  return new String(res);          // A string containing the characters of res
}
```

8.3   Multidimensional Arrays

The types of multidimensional arrays are written `t[][]`, `t[][][]`, and so on. A rectangular *n*-dimensional array of size $\ell_1 \times \ell_2 \times \cdots \times \ell_n$ is created (allocated) using the array creation expression

```
new t[ℓ1][ℓ2]...[ℓn]
```

A multidimensional array a of type `t[][]` is in fact a one-dimensional array of arrays; its component arrays have type `t[]`. Hence a multidimensional array need not be rectangular, and one need not create all the dimensions at once. To create only the first *k* dimensions of size $\ell_1 \times \ell_2 \times \cdots \times \ell_k$ of an *n*-dimensional array, leave the $(n-k)$ last brackets empty:

```
new t[ℓ1][ℓ2]...[ℓk][]...[]
```

To access an element of an *n*-dimensional array a, use *n* index expressions: `a[i1][i2]...[in]`.

8.4   The Utility Class Arrays

Class Arrays from package `java.util` provides static utility methods to compare, fill, sort, and search arrays, and to create a collection (chapter 22) from an array. The `binarySearch`, `equals`, `fill`, and `sort` methods are overloaded also on arrays of type `byte`, `char`, `short`, `int`, `long`, `float`, `double`, `Object`; and `equals` and `fill` also on type `boolean`. The Object versions of `binarySearch` and `sort` use the `compareTo` method of the array elements, unless an explicit Comparator object (section 22.8) is given.

- `static List<T> asList(T... a)` returns a List<T> view (section 22.2) of the elements of parameter array a, in index order. The resulting list implements interface RandomAccess.
- `static int binarySearch(byte[] a, byte k)` returns an index `i>=0` for which `a[i]==k`, if any; otherwise returns `i<0` such that `(-i-1)` would be the proper position for k. The array a must be sorted, as by `sort(a)`, or else the result is undefined.
- `static int binarySearch(Object[] a, Object k)` works like the preceding method, but compares array elements using their `compareTo` method (section 22.8 and example 122).
- `static int binarySearch(Object[] a, Object k, Comparator cmp)` works like the preceding method, but compares array elements using the method `cmp.compare` (section 22.8).
- `static boolean equals(byte[] a1, byte[] a2)` returns `true` if a1 and a2 have the same length and contain the same elements, in the same order.
- `static boolean equals(Object[] a1, Object[] a2)` works like the preceding method, but compares array elements using their `equals` method (section 22.8).
- `static void fill(byte[] a, byte v)` sets all elements of a to v.
- `static void fill(byte[] a, int from, int to, byte v)` sets `a[from..(to-1)]` to v.
- `static void sort(byte[] a)` sorts the array a using quicksort, which is not stable.
- `static void sort(Object[] a)` sorts the array a using mergesort, which is stable. Elements are compared using their `compareTo` method (section 22.8).
- `static void sort(T[] a, Comparator<? extends T> cmp)` works like the preceding method, but elements are compared using the method `cmp.compare` (section 22.8). Is stable.
- `static void sort(byte[] a, int from, int to)` sorts `a[from..(to-1)]`.

Example 22 Creating Multidimensional Arrays
Consider this rectangular 3-by-2 array and this two-dimensional "jagged" (lower triangular) array:

```
0.0   0.0              0.0
0.0   0.0              0.0   0.0
0.0   0.0              0.0   0.0   0.0
```

The following program shows two ways (r1, r2) to create the rectangular array, and three ways (t1, t2, t3) to create the "jagged" array:

```
double[][] r1 = new double[3][2];
double[][] r2 = new double[3][];
for (int i=0; i<3; i++)
  r2[i] = new double[2];

double[][] t1 = new double[3][];
for (int i=0; i<3; i++)
  t1[i] = new double[i+1];
double[][] t2 = { { 0.0 }, { 0.0, 0.0 }, { 0.0, 0.0, 0.0 } };
double[][] t3 = new double[][] { { 0.0 }, { 0.0, 0.0 }, { 0.0, 0.0, 0.0 } };
```

Example 23 Using Multidimensional Arrays
The genetic material of living organisms is held in DNA, conceptually a string AGCTTTTCA of nucleotides A, C, G, and T. A triple of nucleotides, such as AGC, is called a codon; a codon may code for an amino acid. This program counts the frequencies of the $4 \cdot 4 \cdot 4 = 64$ possible codons, using a three-dimensional array freq. The auxiliary array fromNuc translates from the nucleotide letters (A,C,G,T) to the indexes (0,1,2,3) used in freq. The array toNuc translates from indexes to nucleotide letters when printing the frequencies.

```
static void codonfreq(String s) {
  int[] fromNuc = new int[128];
  for (int i=0; i<fromNuc.length; i++)
    fromNuc[i] = -1;
  fromNuc['a'] = fromNuc['A'] = 0; fromNuc['c'] = fromNuc['C'] = 1;
  fromNuc['g'] = fromNuc['G'] = 2; fromNuc['t'] = fromNuc['T'] = 3;
  int[][][] freq = new int[4][4][4];
  for (int i=0; i+2<s.length(); i+=3) {
    int nuc1 = fromNuc[s.charAt(i)];
    int nuc2 = fromNuc[s.charAt(i+1)];
    int nuc3 = fromNuc[s.charAt(i+2)];
    freq[nuc1][nuc2][nuc3] += 1;
  }
  final char[] toNuc = { 'A', 'C', 'G', 'T' };
  for (int i=0; i<4; i++)
    for (int j=0; j<4; j++) {
      for (int k=0; k<4; k++)
        System.out.print(" "+toNuc[i]+toNuc[j]+toNuc[k]+": " + freq[i][j][k]);
      System.out.println();
    }
}
```

9 Classes

9.1 Class Declarations and Class Bodies

A *class-declaration* of class C has the form

> *class-modifiers* `class` C *extends-clause implements-clause*
>   *class-body*

A declaration of class C introduces a new reference type C. The *class-body* may contain declarations of fields, constructors, methods, nested classes, nested interfaces, and initializer blocks. A class declaration may take type parameters and be generic; see section 21.4. The declarations in a class may appear in any order:

> {
>   *field-declarations*
>   *constructor-declarations*
>   *method-declarations*
>   *class-declarations*
>   *interface-declarations*
>   *enum-type-declaration*
>   *initializer-blocks*
> }

A field, method, nested class, nested interface, or nested enum type is called a *member* of the class. A member may be declared `static`. A non-static member is also called an *instance member*.

The scope of a member is the entire class body, except where shadowed by a variable or parameter or by a member of a nested class or interface. The scope of a (static) field does not include (static) initializers preceding its declaration, but the scope of a static field does include all non-static initializers. There can be no two nested classes or interfaces or enum types with the same name, and no two fields with the same name, but a field, a method and a class (or interface or enum type) may have the same name.

By *static code* we mean expressions and statements in static field initializers, static initializer blocks, and static methods. By *non-static code* we mean expressions and statements in constructors, non-static field initializers, non-static initializer blocks, and non-static methods. Non-static code is executed inside a *current object*, which can be referred to as `this` (section 11.10). Static code cannot refer to non-static members or to `this`, only to static members.

9.2 Top-Level Classes, Nested Classes, Member Classes, and Local Classes

A *top-level class* is a class declared outside any other class or interface declaration. A *nested class* is a class declared inside another class or interface. There are two kinds of nested classes: a *local class* is declared inside a method or constructor or initializer block; a *member class* is not. A non-static member class, or a local class in a non-static member, is called an *inner class*, because an object of the inner class will contain a reference to an object of the enclosing class. See also section 9.11.

9.3 Class Modifiers

For a top-level class, the *class-modifiers* may be a list of `public` and at most one of `abstract` and `final`. For a member class, they may be a list of `static`, and at most one of `abstract` and `final`, and at most one of `private`, `protected`, and `public`. For a local class, they may be at most one of `abstract` and `final`.

Example 24 Class Declaration
The Point class is declared to have two non-static fields x and y, one constructor, and two non-static methods.
It is used in examples 12 and 49.

```
class Point {
  int x, y;

  Point(int x, int y) { this.x = x; this.y = y; }

  void move(int dx, int dy) { x += dx; y += dy; }

  public String toString() { return "(" + x + ", " + y + ")"; }
}
```

Example 25 Class with Static and Non-static Members
The SPoint class declares a static field `allpoints` and two non-static fields x and y. Thus each SPoint object
has its own x and y fields, but all objects share the same `allpoints` field in the SPoint class.

The constructor inserts the new object (`this`) into the ArrayList object `allpoints` (section 22.2). The
non-static method `getIndex` returns the point's index in the array list. The static method `getSize` returns the
number of SPoints created so far. The static method `getPoint` returns the i'th SPoint in the array list. Class
SPoint is used in example 56.

```
class SPoint {
  static ArrayList<SPoint> allpoints = new ArrayList<SPoint>();
  int x, y;

  SPoint(int x, int y) { allpoints.add(this); this.x = x; this.y = y; }
  void move(int dx, int dy) { x += dx; y += dy; }
  public String toString() { return "(" + x + ", " + y + ")"; }
  int getIndex() { return allpoints.indexOf(this); }
  static int getSize() { return allpoints.size(); }
  static SPoint getPoint(int i) { return allpoints.get(i); }
}
```

Example 26 Top-Level, Member, and Local Classes
See also examples 39 and 44.

```
class TLC {                         // Top-level class TLC
  static class SMC { ... }          // Static member class

  class NMC { ... }                 // Non-static member (inner) class

  void nm() {                       // Non-static method in TLC
    class NLC { ... }               // Local (inner) class in method
  }

  static void sm() {                // Static method in TLC
    class SLC { ... }               // Local class in method
  }
}
```

9.4   The Class Modifiers `public`, `final`, `abstract`

If a top-level class C is declared `public`, then it is accessible also outside its package (chapter 18).

If a class C is declared `final`, one cannot declare subclasses of C and hence cannot override any methods declared in C. This is useful for preventing rogue subclasses from violating data representation invariants.

If a class C is declared `abstract`, then it cannot be instantiated, but non-abstract subclasses of C can be instantiated. An abstract class may declare constructors and have initializers, to be executed when instantiating non-abstract subclasses. An abstract class may declare abstract and non-abstract methods; a non-abstract class cannot declare abstract methods. A class cannot be both `abstract` and `final`, because no objects could be created of that class.

9.5   Subclasses, Superclasses, Class Hierarchy, Inheritance, and Overriding

A class C may be declared as a *subclass* of class B by an *extends-clause* of the form

```
class C extends B { ... }
```

Class C is a subclass and hence a subtype (section 5.5) of B and its supertypes. It inherits all methods and fields (even private ones, although they are not accessible in class C), but not the constructors, from B.

Class B is called the *immediate superclass* of C. A class can have at most one immediate superclass. The predefined class Object is a superclass of all other classes and has no superclass, so the classes form a *class hierarchy* in which every class is a descendant of its immediate superclass, except Object, which is at the top.

The very first action of a constructor in C may be an explicit call to a constructor in superclass B, like this:

super (*actual-list*) ;   or   o.super (*actual-list*) ;

A superclass constructor call may appear only at the very beginning of a constructor body. The second form o.super (*actual-list*) is used when C's superclass B is an inner class. In that case the new C-object needs an enclosing object (sections 9.11 and 10.3); the value of o is that enclosing object and must not be `null`.

If a constructor C(...) in subclass C does not explicitly call super(...) as its first action, then it implicitly calls the argumentless *default constructor* B() in superclass B as its first action, as if by super(). In this case, B must have a non-private argumentless constructor B(). Conversely, if there is no argumentless constructor B() in B, then C(...) in C must use super(...) to explicitly call some other constructor in B.

The declaration of C may *override* a non-final non-static method m inherited from B by declaring a new non-static method m with the exact same signature. An overridden B-method m can be referred to as super.m inside C's constructors, non-static methods, and non-static initializers. The overriding method m in C

- must be at least as accessible (section 9.7) as the overridden method in B;
- must have the same signature (disregarding `final`) as the overridden method in B; and must have a return type that is a subtype of that of the overridden method in B;
- either has no *throws-clause*, or has a *throws-clause* that covers no more checked exception classes than the *throws-clause* (if any) of the overridden method in B.

The declaration of C may *hide* a non-final static method m inherited from B by declaring a new static method m with the exact same signature. It is illegal for a static method to hide a non-static one, and vice versa.

The declaration of C may *hide* a non-static field f inherited from B by declaring an additional non-static field of the same name (see section 9.6 and examples 30, 43 and 53). The hidden instance field f inherited from B can be referred to as super.f inside C's constructors, non-static methods, and non-static initializers.

Example 27 Abstract Classes, Subclasses, and Overriding
The abstract class Vessel models the notion of a vessel (for holding liquids): it has a field `contents` representing its actual contents, an abstract method `capacity` for computing its maximal capacity, and a method for filling in more, but only up to its capacity (the excess will be lost). The abstract class has subclasses Tank (a rectangular vessel), Cube (a cubic vessel, subclass of Tank), and Barrel (a cylindrical vessel).

The subclasses implement the `capacity` method, they inherit the `contents` field and the `fill` method from the superclass, and they override the `toString` method (inherited from class Object) to print each vessel object appropriately.

```
abstract class Vessel {
  double contents;
  abstract double capacity();
  void fill(double amount) { contents = Math.min(contents + amount, capacity()); }
}
class Tank extends Vessel {
  double length, width, height;
  Tank(double length, double width, double height)
  { this.length = length; this.width = width; this.height = height; }
  double capacity() { return length * width * height; }
  public String toString()
  { return "tank (" + length + ", " + width + ", " + height + ")"; }
}
class Cube extends Tank {
  Cube(double side) { super(side, side, side); }
  public String toString() { return "cube (" + length + ")"; }
}
class Barrel extends Vessel {
  double radius, height;
  Barrel(double radius, double height) { this.radius = radius; this.height = height; }
  double capacity() { return height * Math.PI * radius * radius; }
  public String toString() { return "barrel (" + radius + ", " + height + ")"; }
}
```

Example 28 Using the Vessel Hierarchy from Example 27
The call `vs[i].capacity()` is legal only because the method `capacity`, although abstract, is declared in class Vessel (example 27):

```
public static void main(String[] args) {
  Vessel v1 = new Barrel(3, 10);
  Vessel v2 = new Tank(10, 20, 12);
  Vessel v3 = new Cube(4);
  Vessel[] vs = { v1, v2, v3 };
  v1.fill(90); v1.fill(10); v2.fill(100); v3.fill(80);
  double sum = 0;
  for (int i=0; i<vs.length; i++)
    sum += vs[i].capacity();
  System.out.println("Total capacity is " + sum);
  for (int i=0; i<vs.length; i++)
    System.out.println("vessel number " + i + ": " + vs[i]);
}
```

9.6   Field Declarations in Classes

The purpose of a *field* is to hold a value inside an object (if non-static) or a class (if static). A field must be declared in a class declaration. A *field-declaration* has one of the forms

>   *field-modifiers type fieldname1, fieldname2,* ... ;
>   *field-modifiers type fieldname1 = initializer1,* ... ;

The *field-modifiers* may be a list of the modifiers static, final, transient (section 23.12) and volatile and at most one of the access modifiers private, protected, and public (section 9.7).

If a field f in class C is declared static, then f is associated with the class C and can be referred to independently of any objects of class C. The field can be referred to as C.f or o.f, where o is an expression of type C, or, in the declaration of C, as f. If a field f in class C is not declared static, then f is associated with an *object* (also called *instance*) of class C, and every instance has its own copy of the field. The field can be referred to as o.f, where o is an expression of type C, or, in non-static code in the declaration of C, as f.

If a field f in class C is declared final, the field cannot be modified after initialization. If f has reference type and points to an object or array, the object's fields or the array's elements may still be modified. The initialization must happen either in the declaration or in an initializer block (section 9.13), or if the field is non-static, precisely once in every constructor in class C.

A *field initializer* may be an expression or an array initializer (section 8.2). A static field initializer can refer only to static members of C and can throw no checked exceptions (chapter 15).

A field is given a *default initial value* depending on its type t. If t is a primitive type, the field is initialized to 0 (when t is byte, char, short, int, or long) or 0.0 (when t is float or double) or false (when t is boolean). If t is a reference type, the field is initialized to null.

Static fields are initialized when the class is loaded. First all static fields are given their default initial values, then the static initializer blocks (section 9.13) and static field initializers are executed, in order of appearance in the class declaration.

Non-static fields are initialized when a constructor is called, at which time all static fields have been initialized already (section 9.10).

If a class C declares a non-static field f, and C is a subclass of a class B that has a non-static field f, then every object of class C has two fields, both called f: one is the B-field f declared in the superclass B, and one is the C-field f declared in C itself. What field is referred to by a field access o.f is determined by the compile-time type of o (section 11.9).

9.7   The Member Access Modifiers private, protected, public

A member (field or method or nested class or interface) is always accessible in the class in which it is declared, except where shadowed by a variable or parameter or field (of a nested class). The *access modifiers* private, protected, and public determine where else the member is accessible.

If a member is declared private in top-level class C or a nested class within C, it is accessible in C and its nested classes, but not in their subclasses outside C nor in other classes. If a member in class C is declared protected, it is accessible in all classes in the same package (chapter 18) as C and in subclasses of C, but not in non-subclasses in other packages. If a member in class C is not declared private, protected, or public, it has *package access*, or *default access*, and is accessible only in classes within the same package as C, not in classes in other packages. If a member in class C is declared public, it is accessible in all classes, including classes in other packages. Thus, in order of increasing accessibility, we have private access, package (or default) access, protected access, and public access.

Example 29 Field Declarations
The SPoint class (example 25) declares a static field `allpoints` and two non-static fields x and y.

Example 38 declares a static field `ps` of array type `double[]`. Its field initializer allocates a six-element array and binds it to `ps`, and then the initializer block (section 9.13) stores some numbers into the array.

The Barrel class in example 96 declares two non-static fields `radius` and `height`. The fields are final and therefore must be initialized (which is done in the constructor).

Example 30 Several Fields with the Same Name
An object of class C here has two non-static fields called `vf`, one declared in the superclass B and one declared in C itself. Similarly, an object of class D has three non-static fields called `vf`. Class B and class C each have a static field called `sf`. Class D does not declare a static field `sf`, so in class D the name `sf` refers to the static field `sf` in the superclass C. Examples 43 and 53 use these classes.

```
class B                           // One non-static field vf, one static sf
{ int vf; static int sf; B(int i) { vf = i; sf = i+1; } }

class C extends B                 // Two non-static fields vf, one static sf
{ int vf; static int sf; C(int i) { super(i+20); vf = i; sf = i+2; } }

class D extends C                 // Three non-static fields vf
{ int vf; D(int i) { super(i+40); vf = i; sf = i+4; } }
```

Example 31 Member Access Modifiers
The vessel hierarchy in example 27 is unsatisfactory because everybody can read and modify the fields of a vessel object. Example 96 presents an improved version of the hierarchy in which (1) the `contents` field in Vessel is made private to prevent modification, (2) a new public method `getContents` permits reading the field, and (3) the fields of Tank and Barrel are declared protected to permit access from subclasses declared in other packages.

Since the field `contents` in Vessel is private, it is not accessible in the subclasses (Tank, Barrel, . . .), but the subclasses still inherit the field. Thus every Vessel subclass object has room for storing the field but can change and access it only by using the methods `fill` and `getContents` inherited from the abstract superclass.

Example 32 Private Member Accessibility
A private member is accessible everywhere inside the enclosing top-level class (and only there).

```
class Access {
  private static int x;
  static class SI {
    private static int y = x;     // Access private x from enclosing class
  }
  static void m() {
    int z = SI.y;                 // Access private y from nested class
  }
}
```

9.8   Method Declarations

A *method* must be declared inside a class. A *method-declaration* declaring method m has the form

> *method-modifiers   return-type* m(*formal-list*)   *throws-clause*
>   *method-body*

The *formal-list* is a comma-separated list of zero or more *formal parameter declarations*, of one of the forms

> *parameter-modifier   type   parameter-name*
> *parameter-modifier   type*... *parameter-name*

The *parameter-modifier* may be final, meaning that the parameter cannot be modified inside the method, or absent. The *type* is any type. Each *parameter-name* must be a distinct name. A formal parameter is an initialized variable; its scope is the *method-body*. The second form of parameter declaration can appear only last and declares a parameter array; see section 9.9. For generic methods with type parameters, see section 21.8.

The method name m together with the list $t_1, \ldots, t_n$ of declared parameter types in the *formal-list* determine the *method signature* m($t_1, \ldots, t_n$), where any generic types in $t_1, \ldots, t_n$ are replaced by the underlying non-generic raw types (section 21.11). The *return-type* is not part of the method signature.

A class may declare more than one method with the same *method-name*, provided they have different signatures (after replacing generic types by raw types). This is called *overloading* of the *method-name*.

The *method-body* is a *block-statement* (section 12.2) and thus may contain statements as well as declarations of variables and local classes. In particular, the *method-body* may contain return statements. If the *return-type* is void, the method does not return a value, and no return statement in the *method-body* can have an expression argument. If the *return-type* is not void but a type, the method must return a value: it must not be possible for execution to reach the end of *method-body* without executing a return statement. Moreover, every return statement must have an expression argument whose type is a subtype of the *return-type*.

The *method-modifiers* may be abstract or a list of static, final, synchronized (section 16.2), and at most one of the access modifiers private, protected, and public (section 9.7).

If a method m in class C is declared static, then m is associated with the class C; it can be referred to without any object. The method may be called as C.m(...) or as o.m(...), where o is an expression whose type is a subtype of C, or, inside methods, constructors, field initializers, and initializer blocks in C, simply as m(...). A static method can refer only to static fields and methods of the class.

If a method m in class C is not declared static, then m is associated with an object (instance) of class C. Outside the class, the method must be called as o.m(...), where o is an object of class C or a subclass, or, inside non-static methods, non-static field initializers, and non-static initializer blocks in C, simply as m(...). A non-static method can refer to all fields and methods of class C, whether they are static or not.

If a method m in class C is declared final, it cannot be overridden (redefined) in subclasses.

If a method m in class C is declared abstract, class C must itself be abstract (and so cannot be instantiated). An abstract method cannot be static, final, or synchronized, and its declaration has no method body:

> abstract *method-modifiers return-type* m(*formal-list*) *throws-clause*;

The *throws-clause* of a method or constructor has the form

> throws E1, ..., En

where E1, ..., En are the names of exception types covering all the checked exceptions that the method or constructor may throw. If execution may throw exception e, then e is either an unchecked exception (chapter 15) or a checked exception whose class is a subtype of one of E1, ..., En (which cannot be generic types).

Example 33 Method Name Overloading and Signatures

This class declares four overloaded methods m with signatures m(int) and m(boolean) and m(int, double) and m(double, double); see section 5.6. Some of the overloaded methods are static, others non-static. The overloaded methods may have different return types, as shown here. Example 58 explains the method calls.

It would be legal to declare an additional method with signature m(double, int), but then the method call m(10, 20) would become ambiguous and illegal. Namely, its call signature would be m(int,int) and there is no way to determine whether to call m(int, double) or m(double, int).

```
double m(int i) { return i; }
boolean m(boolean b) { return !b; }
static double m(int x, double y) { return x + y + 1; }
static double m(double x, double y) { return x + y + 3; }
public static void main(String[] args) {
  System.out.println(m(10, 20));          // Prints: 31.0
  System.out.println(m(10, 20.0));        // Prints: 31.0
  System.out.println(m(10.0, 20));        // Prints: 33.0
  System.out.println(m(10.0, 20.0));      // Prints: 33.0
}
```

Example 34 Method Overloading, Overriding, and Hiding

Class C1 declares overloaded method m1 with signatures m1(double) and m1(int) and method m2 with signature m2(int). Its subclass C2 hides C1's static method m1(double) and overloads m2 by declaring additional overloaded variants. These methods are used in example 59.

```
class C1 {
  static void m1(double d) { System.out.println("11d"); }
  void m1(int i) { System.out.println("11i"); }
  void m2(int i) { System.out.println("12i"); }
}
class C2 extends C1 {
  static void m1(double d) { System.out.println("21d"); }
  void m1(int i) { System.out.println("21i"); }
  void m2(double d) { System.out.println("22d"); }
  void m2(Integer ii) { System.out.println("22ii"); }
  void m3(int i)       { System.out.println("23i"); }
  void m4(Integer ii) { System.out.println("24ii"); }
}
```

Example 35 Method Overloading and a Parameter Array

The first declaration of method max has a parameter array xr of type int [], so the method can be called with any number of arguments greater than one. The first argument gets bound to x and the remaining ones to an array bound to xr. However, a call to max(4, 5) will call the second overload max(int, int), because a method that does not require expansion of a parameter array is preferred over one that does.

```
static int max(int x1, int... xr) {
  int res = x1;
  for (int x : xr)
    res = max(res, x);
  return res;
}
static int max(int x, int y) { return x > y ? x : y; }
```

9.9   Parameter Arrays and Variable-Arity Methods (Java 5.0)

The last parameter of a method may be declared to be a *parameter array*, using the syntax

```
t... x
```

where t is a type, x is a parameter name, and the three dots . . . are part of the concrete syntax. In the method, parameter x will have type t[]. In a call to the method, its actual arguments may either be given as zero or more arguments of type t, in which case x gets bound a new array holding the values of those arguments; or the value may be given by a single array of type t[], in which case x gets bound to that array. The first case is used to declare methods that take a variable number of arguments; see example 35.

In overloading resolution, an explicit overload such as max(int, int) is preferred over an expansion of a formal parameter array such as max(int, int...).

9.10   Constructor Declarations

The purpose of a constructor in class C is to initialize new objects (instances) of the class. A *constructor-declaration* in class C has the form

> *constructor-modifiers* C(*formal-list*) *throws-clause*
>   *constructor-body*

The *constructor-modifiers* may be a list of at most one of private, protected, and public (section 9.7); a constructor cannot be abstract, final, or static. A constructor has no return type.

Constructors may be overloaded in the same way as methods: the *constructor signature* (a list of the parameter types in *formal-list*) is used to distinguish constructors in the same class. A constructor may call another overloaded constructor in the same class using the syntax:

> this(*actual-list*)

but a constructor may not call itself, directly or indirectly. A call this(...) to another constructor, if present, must be the very first action of a constructor, preceding any declaration or statement.

The *constructor-body* is a *block-statement* (section 12.2) and so may contain statements as well as declarations of variables and local classes. The *constructor-body* may contain return statements, but no return statement can take an expression argument.

A class that does not explicitly declare a constructor implicitly declares a public, argumentless *default constructor* whose only (implicit) action is to call the superclass constructor (section 9.5):

```
public C() { super(); }
```

The *throws-clause* of the constructor specifies the checked exceptions that may be thrown by the constructor, in the same manner as for methods (section 9.8).

When new creates a new object in memory (section 11.7), the object's non-static fields are given default initial values according to their type. Then a constructor is called to further initialize the object, and the following happens: First, some superclass constructor is called (explicitly or implicitly, see examples 37 and 60) exactly once, then the non-static field initializers and non-static initializer blocks are executed once in order of appearance in the class declaration, and finally the constructor body (except the explicit superclass constructor call, if any) is executed. The call to a superclass constructor will cause a call to a constructor in its superclass, and so on, until reaching Object().

Example 36 Constructor Overloading; Calling Another Constructor
We add a new constructor to the Point class (example 24), thus overloading its constructors. The old constructor has signature Point(int, int) and the new one Point(Point). The new constructor makes a copy of the point p by calling the old constructor using the syntax this(p.x, p.y).

```
class Point {
  int x, y;

  Point(int x, int y)                // Overloaded constructor
  { this.x = x; this.y = y; }

  Point(Point p)                     // Overloaded constructor
  { this(p.x, p.y); }                // Calls the first constructor

  void move(int dx, int dy)
  { x += dx; y += dy; }

  public String toString()
  { return "(" + x + ", " + y + ")"; }
}
```

Example 37 Calling a Superclass Constructor
The constructor in the ColoredPoint subclass (example 86) calls its superclass constructor using the syntax super(x, y).

Example 38 Field Initializers and Initializer Blocks
Here the static field initializer allocates an array and binds it to field ps. The static initializer block fills the array with an increasing sequence of pseudo-random numbers, then scales them so that the last number is 1.0 (this is useful for generating rolls of a random loaded die). This cannot be done using the field initializer alone.

One could delete the two occurrences of static to obtain another example, with a non-static field ps, a non-static field initializer, and a non-static initializer block. However, non-static fields are usually initialized by a constructor.

```
class InitializerExample {
  static double[] ps = new double[6];

  static {                              // Static initializer block
    double sum = 0;
    for (int i=0; i<ps.length; i++)     // Fill with increasing random numbers
      ps[i] = sum += Math.random();
    for (int i=0; i<ps.length; i++)     // Scale so last ps element is 1.0
      ps[i] /= sum;
  }
  ...
}
```

9.11   Nested Classes, Member Classes, Local Classes, and Inner Classes

A non-static nested class, that is, a non-static member class NMC or a local class NLC in a non-static member, is called an *inner class*. An object of an inner class always contains a reference to an object of the enclosing class C, called the *enclosing object*. That object can be referred to as C.this in non-static code (example 44), so a non-static member x of the enclosing object can be referred to as C.this.x.

   An inner class or local class cannot have static members. More precisely, all static fields must also be final, and methods and nested classes in an inner class or local class must be non-static.

   A static nested class, that is, a static member class SMC or a local class in a static member, has no enclosing object and cannot refer to non-static members of the enclosing class C. This is the standard restriction on static members of a class (section 9.1). A static member class may itself have static as well as non-static members.

   If a local class refers to variables or formal parameters in the enclosing method or constructor or initializer, those variables or parameters must be final.

9.12   Anonymous Classes

An *anonymous class* is a special kind of local class; hence it must be declared inside a method or constructor or initializer. An anonymous class can be declared, and exactly one instance created, using the special expression syntax

```
new C(actual-list)
   class-body
```

where C is a class name. This creates an anonymous subclass of class C, with the given *class-body* (section 9.1). Moreover, it creates an object of that anonymous subclass and calls the appropriate C constructor with the arguments in *actual-list*, as if by super (*actual-list*). An anonymous class cannot declare its own constructors.

   When I is an interface name, the similar expression syntax

```
new I()
   class-body
```

creates an anonymous local class, with the given *class-body* (section 9.1), that must implement the interface I, and also creates an object of that anonymous class. Note that the parameter list after I must be empty.

9.13   Initializer Blocks, Field Initializers, and Initializers

In addition to field initializers (section 9.6), a class may contain *initializer-blocks*. Initializer blocks may be used when field initializers or constructors do not suffice. We use the term *initializer* to mean field initializers as well as initializer blocks. A *static initializer block* has the form

```
static block-statement
```

The static initializer blocks and field initializers of static fields are executed, in order of appearance in the class declaration, when the class is loaded. A *non-static initializer block* is simply a free-standing *block-statement*.

   An initializer is not allowed to throw a checked exception (chapter 15). If execution of a static initializer throws an (unchecked) exception other than Error or one of its subclasses, that exception is discarded and the exception ExceptionInInitializerError is thrown instead.

Example 39 Member Classes and Local Classes

```
class TLC {                             // Top-level class
  static int sf;
  int nf;
  static class SMC {                    // Static member class
    static int ssf = sf + TLC.sf;       // can have static members
    int snf = sf + TLC.sf;              // cannot use non-static TLC members
  }
  class NMC {                           // Non-static member (inner) class
    int nnf1 = sf + nf;                 // can use non-static TLC members
    int nnf2 = TLC.sf + TLC.this.nf;    // cannot have static members
  }
  void nm() {                           // Non-static method in TLC
    class NLC {                         // Local (inner) class in method
      int m(int p) { return sf+nf+p; }  // can use non-static TLC members
} } }
```

Example 40 An Iterator as a Local Class
Method suffixes returns an object of the local class SuffixIterator, which implements the Iterator interface (section 22.7) to enumerate the non-empty suffixes of the string s:

```
class LocalInnerClassExample {
  public static void main(String[] args) {
    Iterator<String> seq = suffixes(args[0]);
    while (seq.hasNext())
      System.out.println(seq.next());
  }
  static Iterator<String> suffixes(final String s) {
    class SuffixIterator implements Iterator<String> {
      int startindex=0;
      public boolean hasNext() { return startindex < s.length(); }
      public String next() { return s.substring(startindex++); }
      public void remove() { throw new UnsupportedOperationException(); }
    }
    return new SuffixIterator();
} }
```

Example 41 An Iterator as an Anonymous Local Class
Alternatively, we may use an anonymous local class in method suffixes:

```
static Iterator<String> suffixes(final String s) {
  return
    new Iterator<String>() {
        int startindex=0;
        public boolean hasNext() { return startindex < s.length(); }
        public String next() { return s.substring(startindex++); }
        public void remove() { throw new UnsupportedOperationException(); }
      };
}
```

10   Classes and Objects in the Computer

10.1   What Is a Class?

Conceptually, a class represents a concept, a template for creating instances (objects). In the computer, a class is a chunk of memory, set aside once, when the class is loaded at run-time. A class has the following parts:

- The name of the class.
- Room for all the static members of the class.

A class can be drawn as a box. The header `class SPoint` gives the class name, and the box itself contains the static members of the class:

10.2   What Is an Object?

Conceptually, an object is an instance of a concept (a class). In the computer, an object is a chunk of memory, set aside by an object creation expression `new C(...)`; see section 11.7. Every evaluation of an object creation expression `new C(...)` creates a distinct object, with its own chunk of computer memory. An object has the following parts:

- A reference to the run-time *class* `C` of the object; this is the class `C` used when creating the object.
- Room for all the non-static members of the object.

An object can be drawn as a box. The header `: SPoint` gives the object's class (underlined), and the remainder of the box contains the non-static members of the object:

10.3   Inner Objects

When `NMC` is an inner class (a non-static member class, or a local class in non-static code) in a class `C`, then an object of class `NMC` is an *inner object*. In addition to the object's class and the non-static fields, an inner object always contains a reference to an *enclosing object*, which is an object of the innermost enclosing class `C`. The enclosing object reference can be written `C.this` in non-static code in the inner class.

An object of a static nested class `SMC`, on the other hand, contains no reference to an enclosing object.

Example 42 Objects and Classes

This is the computer memory at the end of the main method in example 56, using the SPoint class from example 25. The variables p and s refer to the same object, variable q is null, and variable r refers to the rightmost object.

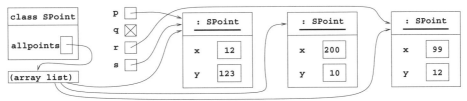

Example 43 Objects With Multiple Fields of the Same Name

This is the computer memory at the end of the main method in example 53, using the classes from example 30. The classes B and C each have a single static field sf; class D has none. The two objects of class C each have two non-static fields vf (called B/vf and C/vf below), and the class D object has three non-static fields vf.

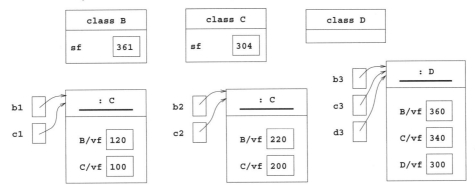

Example 44 Inner Objects

Example 39 declares a class TLC with non-static member (inner) class NMC and static member class SMC. Assume we create a TLC-object, two NMC-objects, and an SMC object:

```
TLC oo = new TLC();
TLC.NMC io1 = oo.new NMC(), io2 = oo.new NMC();
TLC.SMC sio = new TLC.SMC();
```

Then the computer memory will contain these objects (the classes are not shown):

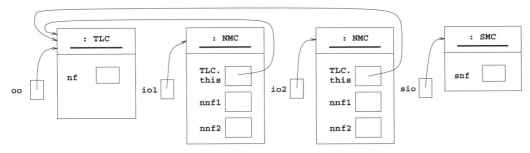

11   Expressions

An expression is evaluated to obtain a value (such as 117). In addition, evaluation of an expression may change the computer's *state*: the values of variables, fields, and array elements, the contents of files, and so on. More precisely, evaluation of an expression either

- terminates normally, producing a value; or

- terminates abruptly by throwing an exception; or

- does not terminate at all (for instance, because it calls a method that does not terminate).

Expressions are built from *literals* (anonymous constants), variables, fields, operators, method calls, array accesses, conditional expressions, the new operator, and so on; see the table of expression forms on the facing page.

One must distinguish the compile-time *type of an expression* from the run-time *class of an object*. An expression has a type (chapter 5) inferred by the compiler. When this is a reference type t, and the value of the expression is an object o, then the class of object o will be a subtype of t but not necessarily equal to t. For instance, the expression (Number)(new Integer(2)) has type Number, but its value is an object whose class is Integer, a subclass of Number.

11.1   Table of Expression Forms

The table of expression forms shows the form, meaning, associativity, argument (operand) types, and result types for expressions. The expressions are grouped according to precedence, as indicated by the horizontal rules, from high precedence to low precedence. Higher-precedence forms are evaluated before lower-precedence forms. Parentheses may be used to emphasize or force a particular order of evaluation.

When an operator (such as +) is left-associative, a sequence e1 + e2 + e3 of operators is evaluated as if parenthesized (e1 + e2) + e3. When an operator (such as =) is right-associative, a sequence e1 = e2 = e3 of operators is evaluated as if parenthesized e1 = (e2 = e3).

In the argument type and result type columns of the table, *integer* stands for any of char, byte, short, int, or long, or their boxed forms Character, Byte, Short, Integer, or Long (section 5.4); and *numeric* stands for integer or float or double, or their boxed forms Float or Double. The type *boolean* stands for boolean or its boxed form Boolean.

For an operator with one integer or numeric operand, the *promotion type* is double if the operand has type double; it is float if the operand has type float; it is long if the operand has type long; otherwise it is int (that is, if the operand has type byte, char, short, or int).

For an operator with two integer or numeric operands (except the shift operators; section 11.4), the promotion type is double if any operand has type double; otherwise, it is float if any operand has type float; otherwise it is long if any operand has type long; otherwise it is int.

Before the operation is performed, the operands are promoted, that is, converted to the promotion type by a widening type conversion (section 5.7).

If the result type is given as numeric also, it equals the promotion type. For example, 10 / 3 has type int, whereas 10 / 3.0 has type double, and c + (byte)1 has type int when c has type char.

Expression	Meaning	Section	Assoc'ty	Argument types	Result type
`a[...]`	array access	8.1		`t[]`, integer	`t`
`o.f`	non-static field access	11.9		object `o`	type of `f`
`C.f`	static field access	11.9			type of `f`
`this`	current object reference	9.1, 11.10			this class
`C.this`	enclosing object reference	9.11, 11.10			`C`
`o.m(...)`	instance method call	11.12		object `o`	return type
`C.m(...)`	static method call	11.12			return type
`super.m(...)`	superclass method call	11.12			return type
`C.super.m(...)`	encl. superclass mth. call	11.12			return type
`t.class`	class object for `t`	24.1		type `t`	`Class<t>`
`x++`	postincrement	11.2		numeric	numeric
`x--`	postdecrement	11.2		numeric	numeric
`++x`	preincrement	11.2		numeric	numeric
`--x`	predecrement	11.2		numeric	numeric
`-x`	negation (minus sign)	11.2	right	numeric	numeric
`~e`	bitwise complement	11.4	right	integer	`int/long`
`!e`	logical negation	11.3	right	boolean	boolean
`new t[...]`	array creation	8.1		type `t`	`t[]`
`new C(...)`	object creation	11.7		class `C`	`C`
`(t)e`	type cast	11.11		type, any	`t`
`e1 * e2`	multiplication	11.2	left	numeric	numeric
`e1 / e2`	division	11.2	left	numeric	numeric
`e1 % e2`	remainder	11.2	left	numeric	numeric
`e1 + e2`	addition	11.2	left	numeric	numeric
`e1 + e2`	string concatenation	7	left	String, any	String
`e1 + e2`	string concatenation	7	left	any, String	String
`e1 - e2`	subtraction	11.2	left	numeric	numeric
`e1 << e2`	left shift	11.4	left	integer	`int/long`
`e1 >> e2`	signed right shift	11.4	left	integer	`int/long`
`e1 >>> e2`	unsigned right shift	11.4	left	integer	`int/long`
`e1 < e2`	less than		none	numeric	boolean
`e1 <= e2`	less than or equal to		none	numeric	boolean
`e1 >= e2`	greater than or equal to		none	numeric	boolean
`e1 > e2`	greater than		none	numeric	boolean
`e instanceof t`	instance test	11.8	none	any, reference type	boolean
`e1 == e2`	equal		left	compatible	boolean
`e1 != e2`	not equal		left	compatible	boolean
`e1 & e2`	bitwise and	11.4	left	integer	`int/long`
`e1 & e2`	logical strict and	11.3	left	boolean	boolean
`e1 ^ e2`	bitwise exclusive-or	11.4	left	integer	`int/long`
`e1 ^ e2`	logical strict exclusive-or	11.3	left	boolean	boolean
`e1	e2`	bitwise or	11.4	left	integer	`int/long`
`e1	e2`	logical strict or	11.3	left	boolean	boolean
`e1 && e2`	logical and	11.3	left	boolean	boolean
`e1 || e2`	logical or	11.3	left	boolean	boolean
`e1 ? e2 : e3`	conditional	11.6	right	boolean, any, any	any
`x = e`	assignment	11.5	right	`e` subtype of `x`	type of `x`
`x += e`	compound assignment	11.5	right	compatible	type of `x`

11.2   Arithmetic Operators

The value of the postincrement expression x++ is that of x, and its effect is to increment x by 1; and similarly for postdecrement x-- which decrements by 1. The value of the preincrement expression ++x is that of x+1, and its effect is to increment x by 1; and similarly for predecrement --x.

Integer division e1/e2 truncates, that is, rounds toward zero, so 10/3 is 3, and (-10)/3 is −3. The integer remainder x%y equals x-(x/y)*y when y is non-zero; it has the same sign as x. Integer division or remainder by zero throws the exception ArithmeticException. Integer overflow does not throw an exception but wraps around. Thus, in the int type, the expression 2147483647+1 evaluates to −2147483648, and the expression -2147483648-1 evaluates to 2147483647.

The floating-point remainder x%y roughly equals x-(((int)(x/y))*y when y is non-zero. Floating-point division by zero and floating-point overflow do not throw exceptions but produce special IEEE754 values (of type float or double) such as Infinity or NaN ("not a number").

11.3   Logical Operators

The operators == and != require the operand types to be compatible: one must be a subtype of the other, possibly after an unboxing operation. Two values of primitive type are equal (by ==) if they represent the same value after conversion to their common supertype. For instance, 10 and 10.0 are equal. Two values of reference type are equal (by ==) if both are null, or both are references to the same object or array, created by the same boxing operation or execution of the new-operator. Hence do not use == or != to compare strings or boxed numbers: two strings s1 and s2 may contain the same sequence of characters and be equal by s1.equals(s2), yet be distinct objects and unequal by s1==s2 (example 8). Similarly for boxed numbers (example 3).

The logical operators && and || perform *shortcut evaluation*: if e1 evaluates to true in e1&&e2, then e2 is evaluated to obtain the value of the expression; otherwise e2 is ignored and the value of the expression is false. Conversely, if e1 evaluates to false in e1||e2, then e2 is evaluated to obtain the value of the expression; otherwise e2 is ignored and the value of the expression is true. By contrast, the operators & (logical strict and) and ^ (logical strict exclusive-or) and | (logical strict or) always evaluate both operands, regardless of the value of the left-hand operand. Usually the shortcut operators && and || are preferable.

11.4   Bitwise Operators and Shift Operators

The operators ~ (bitwise complement, or one's complement) and & (bitwise and) and ^ (bitwise exclusive-or) and | (bitwise or) may be used on operands of integer type. The operators work in parallel on all bits of the 2's complement representation of the operands. Thus ~n equals (-n)-1 and also equals (-1)^n.

The shift operators << and >> and >>> shift the bits of the 2's complement representation of the first argument. The two operands are promoted (section 11.1) separately, and the result type is the promotion type (int or long) of the first argument. Thus the shift operation is always performed on a 32-bit (int) or a 64-bit (long) value. In the former case, the length of the shift is between 0 and 31 as determined by the five least significant bits of the second argument; in the latter case, it is between 0 and 63 as determined by the six least significant bits of the second argument.

The left shift n<<s equals n*2*2*...*2 where there are s multiplications. The signed right shift n>>s of a non-negative n equals n/2/2/.../2 where there are s divisions; the signed right shift of a negative n equals ~((~n)>>s). The unsigned right shift n>>>s of a non-negative n equals n>>s; the signed right shift of a negative n equals (n>>s)+(2<<~s) if n has type int, and (n>>s)+(2L<<~s) if it has type long, where 2L is the long constant with value 2. See example 83 for a "clever" and intricate use of bitwise operators.

Example 45 Arithmetic Operators

```
public static void main(String[] args) {
  int max = 2147483647;
  int min = -2147483648;
  println(max+1);                          // Prints: -2147483648
  println(min-1);                          // Prints:  2147483647
  println(-min);                           // Prints: -2147483648
  print(   10/3); println(   10/(-3));     // Prints:  3 -3
  print((-10)/3); println((-10)/(-3));     // Prints: -3  3
  print(   10%3); println(   10%(-3));     // Prints:  1  1
  print((-10)%3); println((-10)%(-3));     // Prints: -1 -1
}
static void print(int i)   { System.out.print(i + " "); }
static void println(int i) { System.out.println(i + " "); }
```

Example 46 Logical Operators

Because of shortcut evaluation of &&, this expression from example 20 does not evaluate the array access
days[mth-1] unless $1 \leq$ mth ≤ 12, so the index is never out of bounds:

```
(mth >= 1) && (mth <= 12) && (day >= 1) && (day <= days[mth-1])
```

This returns true if y is a leap year, namely, if y is a multiple of 4 but not of 100, or is a multiple of 400:

```
static boolean leapyear(int y)
{ return y % 4 == 0 && y % 100 != 0 || y % 400 == 0; }
```

Example 47 Bitwise Operators and Shift Operators

```
class Bitwise {
  public static void main(String[] args) throws Exception {
    int a = 0x3;                           // Bit pattern   0011
    int b = 0x5;                           // Bit pattern   0101
    println4(a);                           // Prints:       0011
    println4(b);                           // Prints:       0101
    println4(~a);                          // Prints:       1100
    println4(~b);                          // Prints:       1010
    println4(a & b);                       // Prints:       0001
    println4(a ^ b);                       // Prints:       0110
    println4(a | b);                       // Prints:       0111
  }
  static void println4(int n) {
    for (int i=3; i>=0; i--)
      System.out.print(n >> i & 1);
    System.out.println();
  }
}
```

11.5   Assignment Expressions

In the *assignment expression* x = e, the type of e must be a subtype of the type of x, possibly after boxing or unboxing (section 5.4). The type of the expression is the same as the type of x. The assignment is executed by evaluating expression x and then e, and storing e's value in variable x, after a widening conversion (section 11.11) if necessary. When e is a compile-time constant of type byte, char, short, or int, and x has type byte, char, or short, a narrowing conversion is done automatically, provided the value of e is within the range representable in x (section 5.1). The value of the expression x = e is that of x after the assignment.

The assignment operator is right-associative, so x = y = e means x = (y = e).

When e has reference type (object type or array type), only a reference to the object or array is stored in x. Thus the assignment x = e does not copy the object or array (example 49).

When x and e have the same type, the compound assignment x += e is equivalent to x = x + e; however, x is evaluated only once, so in a[i++] += e the variable i is incremented only once. When the type of x is t, different from the type of e, then x += e is equivalent to x = (t)(x + e), in which the intermediate result (x + e) is converted to type t (section 11.11); again x is evaluated only once. The other compound assignment operators -=, *=, and so on, are similar.

Since assignment associates to the right, and the value of sum += e is that of sum after the assignment, one can write ps[i] = sum += e to first increment sum by e and then store the result in ps[i] (example 38).

11.6   Conditional Expressions

The *conditional expression* e1 ? e2 : e3 is legal if e1 has type boolean or Boolean. The type of the conditional expression is the least common supertype of e2 and e3, possibly after boxing operations. The common supertype always exists; for instance, (b ? false : 3.4) has type Object because of boxing to Boolean and Double. The conditional expression is evaluated by first evaluating e1. If e1 evaluates to true, then e2 is evaluated; otherwise e3 is evaluated. The resulting value is the value of the conditional expression.

11.7   Object Creation Expressions

The *object creation expression*

        new C(*actual-list*)

creates a new object of class C and then calls that constructor in class C whose signature matches the arguments in *actual-list*. The *actual-list* is evaluated from left to right to obtain a list of argument values. These argument values are bound to the constructor's parameters, an object of the class is created in the memory, the non-static fields are given default initial values according to their type, a superclass constructor is called explicitly or implicitly (examples 37 and 60), all non-static field initializers and initializer blocks are executed in order of appearance, and finally the constructor body is executed to initialize the object. The value of the constructor call expression is the newly created object, whose class is C.

When C is an inner class in class D, and o evaluates to an object of class D, then one may create a C-object inside o using the syntax o.new C(*actual-list*); see example 44.

11.8   Instance Test Expressions

The *instance test* e instanceof t is evaluated by evaluating e to a value v. If v is not null and is a reference to an object of class C, where C is a subtype of t, the result is true; otherwise false.

Example 48 Widening, Narrowing, and Truncation in Assignments
The assignment d = 12 performs a widening of 12 from int to double. The assignments b = 123 and b2
= 123+1 perform an implicit narrowing from int to byte, because the right-hand sides are compile-time
constants. The assignment b2 = b1+1 would be illegal because b1+1 is not a compile-time constant. The
assignment b2 = 123+5 would be illegal because, although 123+5 is a compile-time constant, its value is not
representable as a byte (whose range is −128..127).

```
double d;
d = 12;                    // Widening conversion from int to double
byte b1 = 123;             // Narrowing conversion from int to byte
byte b2;
b2 = 123 + 1;              // Legal: 123+1 is a compile-time constant
b2 = (byte)(b1 + 1);       // Legal: (byte)(b1 + 1) has type byte
int x = 0;
x += 1.5;                  // Equivalent to: x = (int)(x + 1.5); thus adds 1 to x
```

Example 49 Assignment Does Not Copy Objects
This example uses the Point class from example 24. Assignment (and parameter passing) copies only the
reference, not the object:

```
Point p1 = new Point(10, 20);
System.out.println("p1 is " + p1);      // Prints: p1 is (10, 20)
Point p2 = p1;                          // p1 and p2 refer to same object
p2.move(8, 8);
System.out.println("p2 is " + p2);      // Prints: p2 is (18, 28)
System.out.println("p1 is " + p1);      // Prints: p1 is (18, 28)
```

Example 50 Compound Assignment Operators
Compute the product of all elements of array xs:

```
static double multiply(double[] xs) {
  double prod = 1.0;
  for (int i=0; i<xs.length; i++)
    prod *= xs[i];                      // Equivalent to: prod = prod * xs[i]
  return prod;
}
```

Example 51 Conditional Expression
Return the absolute value of x (always non-negative):

```
static double absolute(double x)
{ return (x >= 0 ? x : -x); }
```

Example 52 Object Creation and Instance Test

```
Number n1 = new Integer(17);
Number n2 = new Double(3.14);
// The following statements print: false, true, false, true.
System.out.println("n1 is a Double:   " + (n1 instanceof Double));
System.out.println("n2 is a Double:   " + (n2 instanceof Double));
System.out.println("null is a Double: " + (null instanceof Double));
System.out.println("n2 is a Number:   " + (n2 instanceof Number));
```

11.9   Field Access Expressions

A *field access* must have one of these three forms:

```
f
C.f
o.f
```

where C is a class and o an expression of reference type.

A class may have several fields of the same name f (section 9.6, example 30, and example 53).

A field access f must refer to a static or non-static field declared in or inherited by a class whose declaration encloses the field access expression (when f has not been shadowed by a field in a nested enclosing class, or by a variable or parameter of the same name). The class declaring the field is the target class TC.

A field access C.f must refer to a static field in class C or a superclass of C. That class is the target class TC.

A field access o.f, where expression o has type C, must refer to a static or non-static field in class C or a superclass of C. That class is the target class TC. To evaluate the field access, the expression o is evaluated to obtain an object. If the field is static, the object is ignored and the value of o.f is the TC-field f. If the field is non-static, the value of o must be non-null and the value of o.f is the value of the TC-field f in object o.

It is informative to contrast a non-static field access and a non-static method call (section 11.12):

- In a non-static field access o.f, the field referred to is determined by the compile-time *type* of the object expression o.

- In a non-static call to a non-private method o.m(...), the method called is determined by the run-time *class* of the target object: the object to which o evaluates.

11.10   The Current Object Reference `this`

The name this may be used in non-static code to refer to the current object (section 9.1). When non-static code in a given object is executed, the object reference this refers to the object as a whole. Hence, when f is a field and m is a method (declared in the innermost enclosing class), then this.f means the same as f (when f has not been shadowed by a variable or parameter of the same name), and this.m(...) means the same as m(...).

When D is an inner class in an enclosing class C, then inside D the notation C.this refers to the C object enclosing the inner D object. See example 39 where TLC.this.nf refers to field nf of the enclosing class TLC.

11.11   Type Cast Expression

A *type cast* of expression e to t is done using this expression, which has type t:

```
(t)e
```

When e is an expression of primitive type and t is a primitive type, the cast is a widening or narrowing conversion (section 5.7). When t is a primitive type and e has the corresponding boxed type, the cast is an unboxing, and when e has primitive type and t is the corresponding boxed type, it is a boxing (section 5.4).

When e is an expression of reference type and t is a reference type, the type cast is evaluated by evaluating e to a value v. If v is null or is a reference to an object or array whose class is a subtype of t, then the type cast succeeds with result v; otherwise the exception ClassCastException is thrown. The type cast is illegal when it cannot possibly succeed at run-time, for instance, when e has type Double and t is Boolean.

Example 53 Field Access
Here we illustrate static and non-static field access in the classes B, C, and D from example 30. Note that the field referred to by an expression of form o.vf or o.sf is determined by the type of expression o, not the class of the object to which o evaluates.

```
public static void main(String[] args) {
  C c1 = new C(100);                       // c1 has type C; object has class C
  B b1 = c1;                               // b1 has type B; object has class C
  print(C.sf,  B.sf);                      // Prints: 102 121
  print(c1.sf, b1.sf);                     // Prints: 102 121
  print(c1.vf, b1.vf);                     // Prints: 100 120
  C c2 = new C(200);                       // c2 has type C; object has class C
  B b2 = c2;                               // b2 has type B; object has class C
  print(c2.sf, b2.sf);                     // Prints: 202 221
  print(c2.vf, b2.vf);                     // Prints: 200 220
  print(c1.sf, b1.sf);                     // Prints: 202 221
  print(c1.vf, b1.vf);                     // Prints: 100 120
  D d3 = new D(300);                       // d3 has type D; object has class D
  C c3 = d3;                               // c3 has type C; object has class D
  B b3 = d3;                               // b3 has type B; object has class D
  print(D.sf,  C.sf,  B.sf);               // Prints: 304 304 361
  print(d3.sf, c3.sf, b3.sf);              // Prints: 304 304 361
  print(d3.vf, c3.vf, b3.vf);              // Prints: 300 340 360
}
static void print(int x, int y) { System.out.println(x+" "+y); }
static void print(int x, int y, int z) { System.out.println(x+" "+y+" "+z); }
```

Example 54 Using this When Referring to Shadowed Fields
A common use of this is to refer to fields (this.x and this.y) that have been shadowed by parameters (x and y), especially in constructors, as in the Point class from example 24:

```
class Point {
  int x, y;
  Point(int x, int y) { this.x = x; this.y = y; }
... }
```

Example 55 Using this to Pass the Current Object to a Method
In the SPoint class (example 25), the current object reference this is used in the constructor to add the newly created object to the array list allpoints, and it is used in the method getIndex to look up the current object in the array list:

```
class SPoint {
  static ArrayList<SPoint> allpoints = new ArrayList<SPoint>();
  int x, y;
  SPoint(int x, int y) { allpoints.add(this); this.x = x; this.y = y; }
  int getIndex() { return allpoints.indexOf(this); }
... }
```

11.12 Method Call Expressions

A *method call* expression, or *method invocation*, must have one of these five forms:

> m(*actual-list*)
> super.m(*actual-list*)
> C.m(*actual-list*)
> C.super.m(*actual-list*)
> o.m(*actual-list*)

where m is a method name, C is a class name, and o is an expression of reference type. The *actual-list* is a possibly empty comma-separated list of expressions, called the *arguments* or *actual parameters*. The *call signature* is $csig = m(t_1, \ldots, t_n)$, where $(t_1, \ldots, t_n)$ is the list of types of the *n* arguments in the *actual-list*. The forms super.m(*actual-list*) and C.super.m(*actual-list*) can be used only in non-static code.

Determining what method is actually called by a method call is complicated because (1) method names may be overloaded, each version having a distinct signature; (2) methods may be overridden, that is, reimplemented in subclasses; (3) methods that are non-static and non-private are called by dynamic dispatch, given a target object; and (4) a method call in a nested class may call a method declared in some enclosing class. Moreover, to make the number and types of actual arguments match the method's signature, it may be necessary to take into account (1a) automatic boxing or unboxing of arguments, and (1b) expansion of a parameter array, if any.

Section 11.12.1 describes argument evaluation and parameter passing, when it is clear which method m is being called. Section 11.12.2 describes how to determine which method is being called.

11.12.1 Method Call: Parameter Passing

This section considers the evaluation of a method call m(*actual-list*) when it is clear which method m is called, and focuses on the parameter passing mechanism.

The call is evaluated by evaluating the expressions in the *actual-list* from left to right to obtain the argument values. These argument values are then bound to the corresponding parameters in the method's *formal-list*, in order of appearance. A boxing or unboxing conversion (section 5.4) occurs if necessary, and a widening conversion (section 11.11) occurs if the type of an argument expression is a subtype of the method's corresponding parameter type.

If the last formal parameter x is a parameter array t... (section 9.9), then a new array is created to hold those actual arguments not bound to the preceding parameters, and that array is bound to x.

Java uses *call-by-value* to bind argument values to formal parameters, so the formal parameter holds a copy of the argument value. Thus if the method changes the value of a formal parameter, this change does not affect the argument. For an argument of reference type, the parameter holds a copy of the object reference or array reference, and hence the parameter refers to the same object or array as the actual argument expression. Thus if the method changes that object or array, the changes will be visible after the method returns (example 57).

A non-static method must be called with a target object, for example as o.m(*actual-list*), where the target object is the value of o, or as m(*actual-list*), where the target object is the current object reference this. In either case, during execution of the method body, this will be bound to the target object.

A static method is not called with a target object (and so there is no this reference in a static method).

When the argument values have been bound to the formal parameters, the method body is executed. The value of the method call expression is the value returned by the method if its return type is non-void; otherwise the method call expression has no value. When the method returns, all parameters and local variables in the method are discarded.

Example 56 Calling Non-Overloaded, Non-Overridden Methods

This program uses the SPoint class from example 25. The static methods `getSize` and `getPoint` may be called by prefixing them with the class name SPoint, or by prefixing them with an expression of type SPoint such as q, although the latter is bad style. They may be called before any objects have been created. The non-static method `getIndex` must be called with an object, as in `r.getIndex()`; then the method is executed with the current object reference `this` bound to r.

```
System.out.println("Number of points created: " + SPoint.getSize());
SPoint p = new SPoint(12, 123);
SPoint q = new SPoint(200, 10);
SPoint r = new SPoint(99, 12);
SPoint s = p;
q = null;
System.out.println("Number of points created: " + SPoint.getSize());
System.out.println("Number of points created: " + q.getSize());        // Bad style
System.out.println("r is point number " + r.getIndex());
for (int i=0; i<SPoint.getSize(); i++)
  System.out.println("SPoint number " + i + " is " + SPoint.getPoint(i));
```

Example 57 Parameter Passing Copies References, Not Objects and Arrays

In the method call `m(p, d, a)` shown here, the object reference held in p is copied to parameter pp of m, so p and pp refer to the same object, the integer held in d is copied to dd, and the array reference held in a is copied to aa. At the end of method m, the state of the computer memory is this:

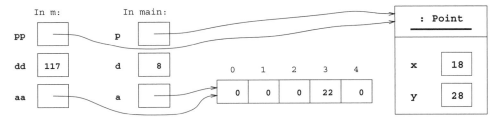

When method m returns, its parameters pp, dd, and aa are discarded. The variables p, d, and a are unmodified, but the object and the array pointed to by p and a have been modified.

```
public static void main(String[] args) {
  Point p = new Point(10, 20);
  int[] a = new int[5];
  int d = 8;
  System.out.println("p is " + p);           // Prints: p is (10, 20)
  System.out.println("a[3] is " + a[3]);      // Prints: a[3] is 0
  m(p, d, a);
  System.out.println("p is " + p);           // Prints: p is (18, 28)
  System.out.println("d is " + d);           // Prints: d is 8
  System.out.println("a[3] is " + a[3]);      // Prints: a[3] is 22
}
static void m(Point pp, int dd, int[] aa) {
  pp.move(dd, dd);
  dd = 117;
  aa[3] = 22;
}
```

11.12.2   Method Call: Determining Which Method Is Called

In general, methods may be overloaded as well as overridden. The overloading is resolved at compile-time by finding the most specific applicable and accessible method signature for the call. Overriding (for non-static methods) is handled at run-time by searching the class hierarchy upwards starting with the run-time class of the object on which the method is called.

At Compile-Time: Determine the Target Type and Signature

Find the target type TC. If the method call has the form m(*actual-list*), the target type TC is the innermost enclosing class containing a method called m that is visible (not shadowed by a method m, regardless of signature, in an intervening class). If the method call has the form super.m(*actual-list*), the target type TC is the superclass of the innermost enclosing class. If the method call has the form C.super.m(*actual-list*), the target type TC is the superclass of the enclosing class C. If the method call has the form C.m(*actual-list*), then TC is C. If the method call has the form o.m(*actual-list*), then TC is the type of the expression o.

Find the target signature tsig. A method in class TC is *applicable* if its signature subsumes the call signature *csig* (section 5.6). Whether a method is *accessible* is determined by its access modifiers (section 9.7). Consider the collection of methods in TC that are both applicable and accessible. The call is illegal (method unknown) if there is no such method. The call is illegal (ambiguous) if there is no method whose signature is most specific, that is, is subsumed by all the others. Thus if the call is legal, there is exactly one most specific signature, the target signature $tsig = m(u_1, \ldots, u_n)$.

Finding the applicable target signatures requires one, two or three stages. In stage 1, automatic boxing/unboxing and parameter arrays are not taken into account when determining whether a method signature subsumes the call signature. If stage 1 finds no applicable signatures, then stage 2 is performed, now taking automatic boxing/unboxing into account. If stage 2 finds no applicable signatures, then stage 3 is performed, taking both automatic boxing/unboxing and parameter array expansion into account. The net effect is a preference for no boxing/unboxing and no parameter array expansion when possible; see examples 35 and 59.

Determine whether the called method is static. If the method call has the form C.m(*actual-list*), the called method must be static. If the method call has the form m(*actual-list*) or o.m(*actual-list*) or super.m(*actual-list*) or C.super.m(*actual-list*), we use the target type TC and the signature *tsig* to determine whether the called method is static or non-static.

At Run-Time: Determine the Target Object (If Non-static) and Execute the Method

If the method is static, no target object is needed: the method to call is the method with signature *tsig* in class TC. When m is static in a method call o.m(*actual-list*), the expression o is evaluated, but its value is ignored.

If the method is non-static, determine the target object; it will be bound to the object reference this during execution of the method. In the case of m(*actual-list*), the target object is this (if TC is the innermost class enclosing the method call), or TC.this (if TC is an outer class containing the method call). In the case of super.m(*actual-list*), the target object is this. In the case of C.super.m(*actual-list*), the target object is C.this. In the case o.m(*actual-list*), the expression o must evaluate to an object reference. If non-null, that object is the target object; otherwise the exception NullPointerException is thrown. If the method is non-private, the class hierarchy is searched to determine which method to call, starting with the class RTC of the target object. If a method with signature *tsig* is not found in class RTC, then the immediate superclass of RTC is searched, and so on. This search procedure is called *dynamic dispatch*. If the method is private, it must be in the target class TC and no search is needed.

When the method has been determined, arguments are evaluated and bound as described in section 11.12.1.

Example 58 Calling Overloaded Methods

Here we call the overloaded methods m declared in example 33. The call m(10, 20) has call signature m(int, int) and calls the method with signature m(int, double), which is the most specific applicable one. The first two lines call the method m(int, double), and the last two call the method m(double, double).

```
System.out.println(m(10, 20));       // Prints: 31.0
System.out.println(m(10, 20.0));     // Prints: 31.0
System.out.println(m(10.0, 20));     // Prints: 33.0
System.out.println(m(10.0, 20.0));   // Prints: 33.0
```

Example 59 Calling Overridden and Overloaded Methods

Here we use the classes C1 and C2 from example 34. The target type of c1.m1(i) is class C1, which has a non-static method with signature m1(int), so the call is to a non-static method; the target object has class C2, so the called method is m1(int) in C2; and quite similarly for c2.m1(i). The target type for c1.m1(d) is the class C1, which has a static method with signature m1(double), so the call is to a static method, and the object bound to c1 does not matter (and calling a static method through an object is bad style). Similarly for c2.m1(d), whose target type is C2, so it calls m1(double) in C2, which overrides m1(double) in C1.

The calls to c2.m2 with arguments of type int and Integer require no boxing or unboxing because there are overloads c2(int) and c2(Integer). The call to m3 involves unboxing and that to m4 involves boxing.

```
int i = 17;
Integer ii = new Integer(i);
double d = 17.0;
C2 c2 = new C2();                           // Type C2, object class C2
C1 c1 = c2;                                 // Type C1, object class C2
c1.m1(i); c2.m1(i); c1.m1(d); c2.m1(d);     // Prints 21i 21i 11d 21d
c1.m2(i);                                   // Prints 12i
c2.m2(i);                                   // Prints 12i,  no boxing/unboxing
c2.m2(ii);                                  // Prints 22ii, no boxing/unboxing
c2.m3(ii);                                  // Prints 23i,  with unboxing
c2.m4(i);                                   // Prints 24ii, with boxing
```

Example 60 Calling Overridden Methods from a Constructor

When d2 is an object of class D2, then d2.m2() calls the method m2 inherited from superclass D1. The call m1() in m2 is equivalent to this.m1(), where this is d2, so the method m1 declared in class D2 is called. Hence d2.m2() prints D1.m2 and D2.m1:7. It prints 7 because field f is initialized to 7 in constructor D2().

Perhaps more surprisingly, the creation d2 = new D2() of an object of class D2 will print D1.m2 and then D2.m1:0. Why does it print 0, not 7? The very first action of constructor D2() is to make an implicit call to the superclass constructor D1(), even *before* executing the assignment f = 7. Hence f will still have its default value 0 when method m1 in D2 is called from method m2 in D1, which in turn is called from constructor D1().

```
class D1 {
  D1() { m2(); }
  void m1() { System.out.println("D1.m1 "); }
  void m2() { System.out.print("D1.m2 "); m1(); }
}
class D2 extends D1 {
  int f;
  D2() { f = 7; }
  void m1() { System.out.println("D2.m1:" + f); }
}
```

12   Statements

A *statement* may change the computer's *state*: the value of variables, fields, array elements, the contents of files, and so on. More precisely, execution of a statement either

- terminates normally (meaning execution will continue with the next statement, if any); or
- terminates abruptly by throwing an exception; or
- exits by executing a `return` statement (if inside a method or constructor); or
- exits a switch or loop by executing a `break` statement (if inside a switch or loop); or
- exits the current iteration of a loop and starts a new iteration by executing a `continue` statement (if inside a loop); or
- does not terminate at all, for instance, by executing `while (true) {}`.

12.1   Expression Statements

An *expression statement* is an *expression* followed by a semicolon:

> *expression* ;

It is executed by evaluating the *expression* and ignoring its value. The only forms of *expression* that may be legally used in this way are assignment expressions (section 11.5), increment and decrement expressions (section 11.2), method call expressions (section 11.12), and object creation expressions (section 11.7).

For example, an assignment statement `x=e;` is an assignment expression `x=e` followed by a semicolon.

Similarly, a method call statement is a method call expression followed by semicolon. The value returned by the method, if any, is discarded; the method is executed only for its side effect.

12.2   Block Statements

A *block-statement* is a sequence of zero or more *statements* or *variable-declarations* or *class-declarations*, in any order, enclosed in braces. Within a block, a variable or class can be used only after its declaration.

> {
>   *variable-declarations*
>   *class-declarations*
>   *statements*
> }

12.3   The Empty Statement

An *empty statement* consists of a semicolon only. It is equivalent to the block statement { } that contains no statements or declarations, and it has no effect at all:

> ;

Example 61 Block Statements

The body of this `main` method, like all method bodies and constructor bodies, is a block statement. It contains a variable declaration, a class declaration, and two further block statements. The two `p1` variables have nothing to do with each other: each block statement introduces its own scope; see section 6.3.

```java
public static void main(String[] args) {
  int offset = 10;
  class Pair {
    public final int fst, snd;
    public Pair(int fst, int snd) { this.fst = fst; this.snd = snd; }
    public String toString() { return String.format("(%d,%d)", fst, snd); }
  }
  {
    Pair p1 = new Pair(10, 10+offset);
    System.out.println(p1);
  }
  {
    Pair p1 = new Pair(200, 300);
    System.out.println(p1);
  }
}
```

Example 62 Empty Statement and Infinite Loop Because of Misplaced Semicolon

Here a misplaced semicolon (`;`) causes the loop body to be an empty statement; the increment `i++` is not part of the loop body. Hence the `while` loop will not terminate but go on forever.

```java
int i=0;
while (i<10);
  i++;
```

Example 63 Single `if-else` Statement

This method behaves the same as `absolute` in example 51.

```java
static double absolute(double x) {
  if (x >= 0)
    return x;
  else
    return -x;
}
```

Example 64 Sequence of `if-else` Statements

We cannot use a switch here, because a switch can work only on integer and enum types. But see example 67.

```java
static int wdayno1(String wday) {
  if      (wday.equals("Monday"))    return 1;
  else if (wday.equals("Tuesday"))   return 2;
  else if (wday.equals("Wednesday")) return 3;
  else if (wday.equals("Thursday"))  return 4;
  else if (wday.equals("Friday"))    return 5;
  else if (wday.equals("Saturday"))  return 6;
  else if (wday.equals("Sunday"))    return 7;
  else return -1;                               // Here used to mean 'not found'
}
```

12.4   Choice Statements

12.4.1   The `if` Statement

An `if` statement has the form

> if ⟨*condition*⟩
>   *truebranch*

The *condition* must have type `boolean` or Boolean, and *truebranch* is a statement. If *condition* evaluates to `true`, then *truebranch* is executed, otherwise not.

12.4.2   The `if-else` Statement

An `if-else` statement has the form:

> if ⟨*condition*⟩
>   *truebranch*
> else
>   *falsebranch*

The *condition* must have type `boolean` or Boolean, and *truebranch* and *falsebranch* are statements. If *condition* evaluates to `true`, then *truebranch* is executed; otherwise *falsebranch* is executed.

The `if-else` statement is illustrated by examples 63 and 64 on the preceding page.

12.4.3   The `switch` Statement

A `switch` statement has the form

> switch ⟨*expression*⟩ {
> case *constant1*: *branch1*
> case *constant2*: *branch2*
>   . . .
> default: *branchn*
> }

The type of *expression* must be `int`, `short`, `char`, `byte`, or a boxed version of these, or an enum type (section 14). Each *constant* must be a *compile-time constant* expression, consisting only of literals, `final` variables, `final` fields declared with explicit field initializers, and operators; or it must be an unqualified enum value. No two *constants* may have the same value. Each *constant* must have a subtype of the type of *expression*.

Each *branch* is preceded by one or more `case` clauses and is a possibly empty sequence of statements, usually terminated by `break` or `return` (if inside a method or constructor) or `continue` (inside a loop). There can be at most one `default` clause, placed anywhere inside the `switch` statement, not necessarily last.

The `switch` statement is executed as follows: The *expression* is evaluated to obtain a value v. If v equals one of the *constants*, then the corresponding *branch* is executed. If v does not equal any of the *constants*, then the *branch* following `default` is executed; if there is no `default` clause, nothing is executed. If a *branch* is not exited by `break` or `return` or `continue`, then execution continues with the next *branch* in the switch regardless of the `case` clauses, until a *branch* exits or the switch ends.

One cannot switch on a value of String type. When the number of cases is small, one may use a sequence of `if` statements instead, as in example 64. When possible, it is better to represent the relevant values using an enum type instead of strings. If one *must* switch on strings, do as in example 67.

Example 65 A switch Statement

Here we could have used a sequence of if-else statements, but a switch is both faster and clearer.

```
static String findCountry(int prefix) {
  switch (prefix) {
  case 1:   return "North America";
  case 44:  return "Great Britain";
  case 45:  return "Denmark";
  case 299: return "Greenland";
  case 46:  return "Sweden";
  case 7:   return "Russia";
  case 972: return "Israel";
  default:  return "Unknown";
  }
}
```

Example 66 A switch Statement on an Enum Type

One can switch on a value m of enum type, here type Month from example 88. Enum members such as Apr and Jun appear unqualified in the case expressions.

```
switch (m) {
case Apr: case Jun: case Sep: case Nov:
  return 30;
case Feb:
  return leapYear(y) ? 29 : 28;
default:
  return 31;
}
```

Example 67 The switch Statement and Strings

To switch on values of String type, such as the name of a weekday entered at run-time, use a hashmap (section 22.5) to map each string to an Integer, and then switch on that. The static final field wdayNumber is a HashMap<String,Integer>, declared and initialized as in example 126. When the string is not in the hashmap, the get method returns null, which is mapped to -1 by the conditional expression and then handled by the default branch.

One drawback of this approach is that it is the programmer's responsibility to maintain consistency between the string array and the case labels (numbers).

```
Integer index = wdayNumber.get(args[0]);
switch (index != null ? index : -1) {
case 0:
  System.out.format("Monday: pay is %.2f%n", 10+7.42*hours);
  break;
case 1: case 2: case 3: case 4:
  System.out.format("Workday: pay is %.2f%n", 7.42*hours);
  break;
case 5: case 6:
  System.out.format("Weekend: pay is %.2f%n", 20+1.25*7.42*hours);
  break;
default:
  System.out.format("Unknown weekday: %s%n", args[0]);
}
```

12.5   Loop Statements

12.5.1   The `for` Statement

A `for` statement has the form

```
for (initialization; condition; step)
    body
```

where *initialization* is a *variable-declaration* (section 6.2) or an *expression*, *condition* is an *expression* of type `boolean` or Boolean, *step* is an *expression*, and *body* is a *statement*. More generally, the *initialization* and *step* may also be comma-separated lists of *expressions*; the expressions in such a list are evaluated from left to right. The *initialization*, *condition*, and *step* may be empty. An empty *condition* is equivalent to `true`. Thus `for (;;)` *body* means "forever execute *body*." The `for` statement is executed as follows:

1. The *initialization* is executed.

2. The *condition* is evaluated. If it is `false`, the loop terminates.

3. If it is `true`, then

    a. The *body* is executed.

    b. The *step* is executed.

    c. Execution continues at (2).

Hence the `for` statement above is equivalent to this statement using `while` (section 12.5.3):

```
initialization
while (condition) {
  body
  step
}
```

12.5.2   Using the `for` Statement on Iterables (Java 5.0)

A variant of the `for` statement can be used to iterate over the values of an iterator:

```
for (tx x : expression)
    body
```

The *expression* must have type Iterable<t> (section 22.7) where t is a subtype of type `tx` or is a boxed version of `tx`, or it must be an array whose element type is a subtype of `tx` or is a boxed version of `tx`. Thus iterators obtained from *expression* will produce elements that can be assigned to x, possibly after an unboxing operation. The *body* must be a statement.

First the *expression* is evaluated to obtain an iterable and its `iterator()` method is called to obtain an iterator. Then the *body* is executed for each element produced by the iterator, with variable x bound to that element, possibly after an unboxing operation. Unlike in C#, variable x is not read-only in the *body*.

It is safe to modify the elements of an array while iterating over the array, but in general modification to an object being iterated over can produce unpredictable effects.

This variant of the `for` statement is sometimes called the foreach statement, but "foreach" is not a keyword and the statement must be written as shown above.

Example 68 Nested for Loops
This program prints a four-line triangle of asterisks (*):

```
for (int i=1; i<=4; i++) {
  for (int j=1; j<=i; j++)
    System.out.print("*");
  System.out.println();
}
```

Example 69 Using the Enhanced for Statement on an Array

```
int[] iarr = { 2, 3, 5, 7, 11 };
int sum = 0;
for (int i : iarr)
  sum += i;
System.out.println(sum);
```

Example 70 Using the Enhanced for Statement on an Iterable
Here the enhanced for statement is used to iterate over the elements of an Iterable<Integer>, that is, a generator of Integer sequences. The method fromTo that creates the iterable is defined in example 131.

Examples 71 and 74 show other ways to iterate over the integer sequence.

```
public static void main(String[] args) {
  for (int i : fromTo(13, 17))
    System.out.println(i);
}
public static Iterable<Integer> fromTo(final int m, final int n) {
  ...
}
}
```

Example 71 Explicitly Going through an Iterable Using for
The enhanced for statement in example 70 is equivalent to this for loop: obtain an iterable by calling fromTo(13, 17), obtain an iterator from the iterable, and then go through the iterator's elements using the iterator's hasNext and next methods. Note that the for loop's *step* is empty; the call to next() in the loop body ensures progress. See also example 74.

```
Iterable<Integer> ible = fromTo(13, 17);
for (Iterator<Integer> iter = ible.iterator(); iter.hasNext(); /* none */) {
  int i = iter.next();
  System.out.println(i);
}
```

12.5.3 The while Statement

A while statement has the form

```
while (condition)
    body
```

where *condition* is an expression of type boolean or Boolean, and *body* is a statement. It is executed as follows:

1. The *condition* is evaluated. If it is false, the loop terminates.
2. If it is true, then
   a. The *body* is executed.
   b. Execution continues at (1).

Just after the while loop, the negation of *condition* must hold (unless the loop is exited by break). This fact provides useful information about the program's state after the loop; see example 72 opposite.

When a *loop invariant* — a property that always holds at the beginning and end of the loop body — is known as well, then one can combine it with the negation of the *condition* to get precise information about the program's state after the while loop. This often helps understanding short but subtle loops; see example 73 opposite.

12.5.4 The do-while Statement

A do-while statement has the form

```
do
    body
while (condition);
```

where *condition* is an expression of type boolean or Boolean, and *body* is a statement. The *body* is executed at least once, because the do-while statement is executed as follows:

1. The *body* is executed.
2. The *condition* is evaluated. If it is false, the loop terminates.
3. If it is true, then execution continues at (1).

Hence the do-while statement above is equivalent to the following statement using while:

```
body
while (condition)
    body
```

So a do-while statement does not test the loop *condition* before the first execution of the loop *body*. Mistakenly using a do-while statement where a while statement should have been used leads to program errors. Such errors are discovered only when some day the program encounters an empty input file, a zero-element result set from a database, or a similar borderline situation.

Therefore you should usually prefer while over do-while. But there are cases where do-while is more natural; see example 75 opposite.

Example 72 Linear Array Search Using a `while` Loop
This method behaves as `wdayno1` in example 64. The negation of the loop condition holds just after the loop; note that together with (`i < wdays.length`) it implies that wday equals `wdays[i]`.

```
static int wdayno2(String wday) {
  int i=0;
  while (i < wdays.length && ! wday.equals(wdays[i]))
    i++;
  // Now i >= wdays.length or wday equals wdays[i]
  if (i < wdays.length)
    return i+1;
  else
    return -1;                            // Here used to mean 'not found'
}
static final String[] wdays =
{ "Monday", "Tuesday", "Wednesday", "Thursday", "Friday", "Saturday", "Sunday" };
```

Example 73 Binary Search of a Sorted Array Using a `while` Loop
Assume arr is sorted and imagine that `arr[-1]` is minus infinity and `arr[arr.length]` is plus infinity; then `arr[a-1]<x<arr[b+1]` is a loop invariant. If the loop terminates (without `return`), then it holds just after the loop that `arr[b]<x<arr[a]`, and so inserting x at `arr[a]` would keep the array sorted. If x is found, return i which is non-negative; if x is not found, return the one's complement ~a which is negative (because a>=0).

```
public static int binarySearch(double[] arr, double x) {
  int a=0, b=arr.length-1;
  while (a<=b) { // Loop invariant: arr[a-1] < x < arr[b+1]
    int i = (a+b)/2;
    if (arr[i] < x)      a = i+1;
    else if (arr[i] > x) b = i-1;
    else                 return i;   // because arr[i] == x
  }
  // Now a>b, in fact a==b+1 and b==a-1, and so arr[b] < x < arr[a]
  return ~a;
}
```

Example 74 Explicitly Going through an Iterable Using `while`
This `while` loop is very similar in structure to the `for` loop in example 71.

```
Iterable<Integer> ible = fromTo(13, 17);
Iterator<Integer> iter = ible.iterator();
while (iter.hasNext()) {
  int i = iter.next();
  System.out.println(i);
}
```

Example 75 Using `do-while` to Roll a Die and Compute Sum Until 5 or 6 Comes Up

```
int sum = 0, eyes;
do {
  eyes = (int)(1 + 6 * Math.random());
  sum += eyes;
} while (eyes < 5);
```

12.6 Returns, Labeled Statements, Exits, and Exceptions

12.6.1 The `return` Statement

The simplest form of a `return` statement, without an expression argument, is

```
return;
```

That form of `return` statement must occur in a method whose return type is `void`, or in a constructor. Execution of the `return` statement exits the method or constructor and continues execution at the place from which the method or constructor was called. Alternatively, a `return` statement may have an expression argument:

```
return expression;
```

That form of `return` statement must occur inside the body of a method (not constructor) whose return type is a supertype or boxed or unboxed version of the type of the *expression*. The `return` statement is executed as follows: First the *expression* is evaluated to some value v. Then it exits the method and continues execution at the method call expression that called the method; the value of that expression will be v, possibly after the application of a widening, boxing, or unboxing conversion.

12.6.2 Labeled Statements

A labeled statement has the form

```
label : statement
```

where *label* is a name. The scope of *label* is *statement*, where it can be used in `break` (section 12.6.3) and `continue` (section 12.6.4). The *label* cannot be reused inside *statement*, except inside a local class.

12.6.3 The `break` Statement

A `break` statement is legal only inside a switch or loop and has one of the forms

```
break;
break label;
```

Executing `break` exits the innermost enclosing switch or loop and continues execution after that switch or loop. Executing `break` *label* exits the enclosing statement that has label *label*, and continues execution after that statement. Such a statement must exist in the innermost enclosing method, constructor, or initializer block.

12.6.4 The `continue` Statement

A `continue` statement is legal only inside a loop and has one of the forms

```
continue;
continue label;
```

Executing `continue` terminates the current iteration of the innermost enclosing loop and continues the execution at the *step* in `for` loops (section 12.5.1) or the *condition* in `while` and `do-while` loops (sections 12.5.3 and 12.5.4). Executing `continue` *label* terminates the current iteration of the enclosing loop that has label *label*, and continues the execution at the *step* or the *condition*. There must be such a loop in the innermost enclosing method or constructor or initializer block.

Example 76 Using return to Terminate a Loop Early
This method behaves the same as wdayno2 in example 72:

```
static int wdayno3(String wday) {
  for (int i=0; i < wdays.length; i++)
    if (wday.equals(wdays[i]))
      return i+1;
  return -1;                              // Here used to mean 'not found'
}
```

Example 77 Using break to Terminate a Loop Early

```
double prod = 1.0;
for (int i=0; i<xs.length; i++) {
  prod *= xs[i];
  if (prod == 0.0)
    break;
}
```

Example 78 Using continue to Start a New Iteration (Not Recommended)
This method decides whether query is a substring of target. When a mismatch between the strings is found,
continue starts the next iteration of the outer for loop, thus incrementing j:

```
static boolean substring1(String query, String target) {
  nextposition:
    for (int j=0; j<=target.length()-query.length(); j++) {
      for (int k=0; k<query.length(); k++)
        if (target.charAt(j+k) != query.charAt(k))
          continue nextposition;
      return true;
    }
  return false;
}
```

Example 79 Using break to Exit a Labeled Statement Block (Not Recommended)
This method behaves as substring1 from example 78. It uses break to exit the entire statement block labeled
thisposition, thus skipping the first return statement and starting a new iteration of the outer for loop:

```
static boolean substring2(String query, String target) {
  for (int j=0; j<=target.length()-query.length(); j++)
    thisposition: {
      for (int k=0; k<query.length(); k++)
        if (target.charAt(j+k) != query.charAt(k))
          break thisposition;
      return true;
    }
  return false;
}
```

12.6.5 The `throw` Statement

A `throw` statement has the form

    throw *expression*;

where the type of the *expression* must be a subtype of class Throwable (chapter 15). The `throw` statement is executed as follows: The *expression* is evaluated to obtain an exception object v. If it is null, then a NullPointerException is thrown; otherwise the exception object v is thrown. Thus a thrown exception is never null. In any case, the enclosing block statement terminates abruptly (chapter 15). The thrown exception may be caught by a dynamically enclosing `try-catch` statement (section 12.6.6). If the exception is not caught, then the entire program execution will be aborted, and information from the exception will be printed on the console (for example, at the command prompt, or in the Java Console inside a Web browser).

12.6.6 The `try-catch-finally` Statement

A `try-catch` statement is used to catch (particular) exceptions thrown by the execution of a block of code. It has the following form:

    try
        body
    catch (E1 x1) *catchbody*₁
    catch (E2 x2) *catchbody*₂
    ...
    finally *finallybody*

where E1, E2, ... are names of exception types, x1, x2, ... are variable names, and *body*, *catchbody*$_i$, and *finallybody* are *block-statements* (section 12.2). There can be zero or more `catch` clauses, and the `finally` clause may be absent, but at least one `catch` or `finally` clause must be present.

We say that Ei matches exception type E if E is a subtype of Ei (possibly equal to Ei).

The `try-catch-finally` statement is executed by executing the *body*. If the execution of the *body* terminates normally, or exits by `return` or `break` or `continue` (when inside a method or constructor or switch or loop), then the `catch` clauses are ignored. If the *body* terminates abruptly by throwing exception e of class E, then the first matching Ei (if any) is located, variable xi is bound to e, and the corresponding *catchbody*$_i$ is executed. The *catchbody*$_i$ may terminate normally, or loop infinitely, or exit by executing `return` or `break` or `continue`, or throw an exception (possibly xi); if there is no `finally` clause, this determines how the entire `try-catch` statement terminates. A thrown exception e is never null (section 12.6.5), so xi is guaranteed not to be null either. If there is no matching Ei, then the entire `try-catch` statement terminates abruptly with exception e.

If there is a `finally` clause, then *finallybody* will be executed regardless of whether the execution of *body* terminated normally, regardless of whether *body* exited by executing `return` or `break` or `continue`, regardless of whether any exception thrown by *body* was caught by a `catch` clause, and regardless of whether the `catch` clause exited by executing `return` or `break` or `continue` or by throwing an exception. If execution of *finallybody* terminates normally, then the entire `try-catch-finally` terminates as determined by *body* (or *catchbody*$_i$, if one was executed and terminated abruptly or exited). If execution of *finallybody* terminates abruptly, then that determines how the entire `try-catch-finally` terminates (example 90).

Example 80 Throwing an Exception to Indicate Failure
Instead of returning the bogus error value -1 as in method wdayno3 (example 76), throw a WeekdayException (example 89). Note the throws clause (section 9.8) in the method header.

```
static int wdayno4(String wday) throws WeekdayException {
  for (int i=0; i < wdays.length; i++)
    if (wday.equals(wdays[i]))
      return i+1;
  throw new WeekdayException(wday);
}
```

Example 81 A try-catch Statement
This example calls the method wdayno4 (example 80) inside a try-catch statement that catches exceptions of class WeekdayException (example 89) and its superclass Exception. The second catch clause will be executed (for example) if the array access args[0] fails because there is no command line argument (since ArrayIndexOutOfBoundsException is a subclass of Exception). If an exception is caught, it is bound to the variable x and printed by an implicit call (chapter 7) to the exception's toString method.

```
public static void main(String[] args) {
  try {
    System.out.println(args[0] + " is weekday number " + wdayno4(args[0]));
  } catch (WeekdayException x) {
    System.out.println("Weekday problem: " + x);
  } catch (Exception x) {
    System.out.println("Other problem: " + x);
  }
}
```

Example 82 A try-finally Statement
This method attempts to read three lines from a text file (section 23.4), each containing a single floating-point number. Regardless of whether anything goes wrong during reading (premature end-of-file, ill-formed number), the finally clause will close the readers before the method returns. It would do so even if the return statement were inside the try block.

```
static double[] readRecord(String filename) throws IOException {
  Reader freader        = new FileReader(filename);
  BufferedReader breader = new BufferedReader(freader);
  double[] res = new double[3];
  try {
    res[0] = new Double(breader.readLine()).doubleValue();
    res[1] = new Double(breader.readLine()).doubleValue();
    res[2] = new Double(breader.readLine()).doubleValue();
  } finally {
    breader.close();
  }
  return res;
}
```

12.7 The `assert` Statement

The `assert` statement has one of the following forms:

```
assert boolean-expression ;
assert boolean-expression : expression ;
```

The *boolean-expression* must have type `boolean` or Boolean. The type of *expression* must be `boolean`, `char`, `double`, `float`, `int`, `long`, or a boxed version of these, or Object.

Under ordinary execution of a program, an `assert` statement has no effect at all. However, assertions may be enabled at run-time by specifying the option `-ea` or `-enableassertions` when executing a program `C` (chapter 17):

```
java -enableassertions C
```

When assertions are enabled at run-time, every execution of the `assert` statement will evaluate the *boolean-expression*. If the result is `true`, program execution continues normally. If the result is `false`, the assertion fails and an AssertionError will be thrown; moreover, in the second form of the `assert` statement, the *expression* will be evaluated and its value will be passed to the appropriate AssertionError constructor. Thus the value of the *expression* will be reported along with the exception in case of assertion failure. This simplifies troubleshooting in a malfunctioning program.

An AssertionError signals the failure of a fundamental assumption in the program and should not be caught by a `try-catch` statement in the program; it should be allowed to propagate to the toplevel.

An `assert` statement can serve two purposes: to document the programmer's assumption about the state at a certain point in the program, and to check (at run-time) that that assumption holds (provided the program is executed using the `enableassertions` option).

One may put an `assert` statement after a particularly complicated piece of code, to check that it has achieved what it was supposed to (example 83).

In a class that has a data representation invariant, one may assert the invariant at the end of every method that could modify the state of the current object (example 84).

One should not use `assert` statements to check the validity of user input or the arguments of public methods or constructors, because the check will be performed only if assertions are enabled at run-time. Instead, use ordinary `if` statements and throw an exception in case of error.

The `assert` statement was introduced in Java 1.4.

Example 83 Using `assert` to Specify and Check the Result of an Algorithm

The integer square root of $x \geq 0$ is an integer y such that $y^2 \leq x$ and $(y+1)^2 > x$. The precondition $x \geq 0$ is always checked, using an `if` statement. The postcondition on y is specified by an `assert` statement, and checked if assertions are enabled at run-time — which is reassuring, given that the correctness of this algorithm is none too obvious. The assertion uses casts to `long` to avoid arithmetic overflow in the `assert` statement.

```
static int sqrt(int x) {  // Algorithm by Borgerding, Hsieh, Ulery
  if (x < 0)
    throw new IllegalArgumentException("sqrt: negative argument");
  int temp, y = 0, b = 0x8000, bshft = 15, v = x;;
  do {
    if (v >= (temp = (y<<1)+b << bshft--)) {
      y += b; v -= temp;
    }
  } while ((b >>= 1) > 0);
  assert (long)y * y <= x && (long)(y+1)*(y+1) > x;
  return y;
}
```

Example 84 Using `assert` to Specify and Check Invariants

A word list is a sequence of words to be formatted as a line of text. Its `length` is the minimum number of characters needed to format the words and the interword spaces, that is, the lengths of the words plus the number of words minus 1. Those methods that change the word list use `assert` statements to specify the invariant on `length`, and to check it if assertions are enabled at run-time.

```
class WordList {
  private LinkedList<String> strings = new LinkedList<String>();
  private int length = -1;              // Invariant: equals word lengths plus inter-word spaces
  public int length() { return length; }

  public void addLast(String s) {
    strings.addLast(s);
    length += 1 + s.length();
    assert length == computeLength() + strings.size() - 1;
  }

  public String removeFirst() {
    String res = strings.removeFirst();
    length -= 1 + res.length();
    assert length == computeLength() + strings.size() - 1;
    return res;
  }

  private int computeLength() { ... } // For checking the invariant only
}
```

An algorithm for formatting a sequence of words into a text with a straight right-hand margin should produce lines res of a specified length `lineWidth`, unless there is only one word on the line or the line is the last one. This requirement can be expressed and checked using an `assert` statement. See the complete example file, available online, for details of the formatting algorithm itself.

```
assert res.length()==lineWidth || wordCount==1 || !wordIter.hasNext();
```

13   Interfaces

13.1   Interface Declarations

An *interface* describes fields and methods but does not implement them. An *interface-declaration* may contain field descriptions, method descriptions, class declarations, and interface declarations, in any order.

> *interface-modifiers* interface I *extends-clause* {
>   *field-descriptions*
>   *method-descriptions*
>   *class-declarations*
>   *interface-declarations*
> }

An interface may be declared at toplevel or inside a class or interface but not inside a method or constructor or initializer. At toplevel, the *interface-modifiers* may be public or absent. A public interface is accessible also outside its package. Inside a class or interface, the *interface-modifiers* may be static (always implicitly understood) and at most one of public, protected, or private. An interface declaration may take type parameters and be generic; see section 21.7.

The *extends-clause* may be absent or have the form

> extends I1, I2, ...

where I1, I2, ... is a non-empty list of interface names. If the *extends-clause* is present, then interface I describes all those members described by I1, I2, ..., and interface I is a *subinterface* (and hence subtype) of I1, I2, ... Interface I can describe additional fields and methods but cannot override inherited members.

A *field-description* in an interface declares a named constant and must have the form

> *field-desc-modifiers type* f = *initializer*;

where *field-desc-modifiers* is a list of static, final, and public, none of which needs to be given explicitly, as all are implicitly understood. The field initializer must be an expression involving only literals and operators, and static members of classes and interfaces.

A *method-description* for method m must have the form

> *method-desc-modifiers return-type* m(*formal-list*) *throws-clause*;

where *method-desc-modifiers* is a list of abstract and public, none of which needs to be given explicitly.

A *class-declaration* inside an interface is always implicitly static and public.

13.2   Classes Implementing Interfaces

A class C may be declared to implement one or more interfaces by an *implements-clause*:

> class C implements I1, I2, ...
>   *class-body*

In this case, C is a subtype (section 5.5) of I1, I2, and so on, and C must declare all the methods described by I1, I2, ... with exactly the prescribed signatures and return types. A class may implement any number of interfaces. Fields, classes, and interfaces declared in I1, I2, ... can be used in class C.

Example 85 Three Interface Declarations
The Colored interface describes method getColor, interface Drawable describes method draw, and Colored-Drawable describes both. The methods are implicitly public.

```
import java.awt.*;
interface Colored { Color getColor(); }
interface Drawable { void draw(Graphics g); }
interface ColoredDrawable extends Colored, Drawable {}
```

Example 86 Classes Implementing Interfaces
The methods getColor and draw must be public as in the interface declarations (example 85).

```
class ColoredPoint extends Point implements Colored {
  Color c;
  ColoredPoint(int x, int y, Color c) { super(x, y); this.c = c; }
  public Color getColor() { return c; }
}

class ColoredDrawablePoint extends ColoredPoint implements ColoredDrawable {
  ColoredDrawablePoint(int x, int y, Color c) { super(x, y, c); }
  public void draw(Graphics g) { g.fillRect(x, y, 1, 1); }
}

class ColoredRectangle implements ColoredDrawable {
  int x1, x2, y1, y2;    // (x1, y1) upper left, (x2, y2) lower right corner
  Color c;

  ColoredRectangle(int x1, int y1, int x2, int y2, Color c)
  { this.x1 = x1; this.y1 = y1; this.x2 = x2; this.y2 = y2; this.c = c; }
  public Color getColor() { return c; }
  public void draw(Graphics g) { g.drawRect(x1, y1, x2-x1, y2-y1); }
}
```

Example 87 Using Interfaces as Types
A Colored value has a getColor method; a ColoredDrawable value has a getColor method and a draw method:

```
static void printcolors(Colored[] cs) {
  for (int i=0; i<cs.length; i++)
    System.out.println(cs[i].getColor().toString());
}

static void draw(Graphics g, ColoredDrawable[] cs) {
  for (int i=0; i<cs.length; i++) {
    g.setColor(cs[i].getColor());
    cs[i].draw(g);
  }
}
```

14 Enum Types (Java 5.0)

An enum type is used to declare distinct enum values; an enum type is a reference type. An *enum-type-declaration* is a specialized form of class declaration that begins with a list of enum value declarations:

```
enum-modifiers enum t implements-clause {
    enum-value-list ;
    field-declarations
    constructor-declarations
    method-declarations
    class-declarations
    interface-declarations
    initializer-blocks
}
```

The declarations of fields, methods, nested types, and initializer blocks are as for ordinary classes (section 9.1); these declarations may appear in any order. In fact, the enum type t is implemented as a class and is a reference type, and there is exactly one instance (object) of that implementation class for each declared enum value.

The *enum-modifiers* control the accessibility of the enum type and follow the same rules as class access modifiers (section 9.3). The modifiers abstract and final cannot be used. An enum type may be declared to implement any number of interfaces, but cannot be declared to have a superclass; it implicitly has the superclass java.lang.Enum<t>. An enum type is implicitly final and cannot be used as a superclass. A nested enum type is implicitly static (the static modifier is allowed but is implicitly understood and not required) and cannot refer to instance fields of an enclosing type.

An enum declaration can declare private constructors only, and an enum value cannot be explicitly created using new t (*actual-list*). Instead enum values are created by the *enum-value-list*, which is a (possibly empty) comma-separated list of enum value declarations. An enum value declaration has the form *enum-value* or *enum-value* (*actual-list*). The first one corresponds to a call to the enum type's argumentless constructor and the second one to a call to the constructor overload appropriate for the enum value's *actual-list*.

A declared enum value has the type t of the enclosing enum type, and is similar to a public static final field. Unlike other reference type values, enum values can be used in switch statements (example 66). The *ordinal value* of an enum value is given by its position in the *enum-value-list*; the first one is zero. There are no predefined conversions between enum values and integers, and no numeric operations such as (+), nor comparisons such as (<), on enum values. A value of an enum type always equals a declared *enum-value*.

Outside an enum declaration, an enum value must be written in its fully qualified form, such as Month.Jan, except in the clauses of a switch statement, where it must be written in unqualified form, such as Jan.

Let v1 and v2 be enum values of the same type; then the following operations are defined:

- v1.ordinal() of type int is the ordinal value of the enum value, such as 3.
- v1.toString() of type String is the declared name of the enum value, such as "Thu".
- v1.compareTo(v2) returns a integer that is negative, zero or positive, according as v1 precedes, equals or follows v2 in the declaring enum value list. That is, it compares v1.ordinal() to v2.ordinal().
- v1==v2 is true if v1 and v2 evaluate to the same enum value; otherwise false.
- The static method values() returns a new array of type t[] holding references to all enum values in the enum type. A new array is created at every call to this method, so an application should call it at most once and cache the result if possible, as shown by example 88 opposite.

Example 88 Representing Weekdays and Months Using Enum Types

When specifying a date it is desirable to use numbers for years (2004), dates (11) and ISO week numbers (28), but symbolic values for weekdays (Sun) and months (Jul). In calendrical calculations it is useful to assign numbers 0–6 to the weekdays (Mon–Sun) and numbers 1–12 to the months (Jan–Dec). This is done in the enum types Day and Month below by declaring suitable methods to convert integers to enum values and back.

The Month enum type declares a field days to hold the number of days in the month (in a non-leap year), and a constructor to initialize the field. It also declares a method succ() that computes the next month. Note the use of reference comparison of enum values in method days(int).

```
enum Day {
  Mon, Tue, Wed, Thu, Fri, Sat, Sun;
  private final static Day[] day = values();        // Cache the array
  public static Day toDay(int n) { return day[n]; }
  public int toInt() { return ordinal(); }
}
enum Month {
  Jan(31), Feb(28), Mar(31), Apr(30), May(31), Jun(30),
  Jul(31), Aug(31), Sep(30), Oct(31), Nov(30), Dec(31);
  private final int days;
  private Month(int days) { this.days = days; }
  private final static Month[] month = values();     // Cache the array
  public int days(int year) {
    return this == Feb && MyDate.leapYear(year) ? 29 : days;
  }
  public static Month toMonth(int n) { return month[n-1]; }
  public int toInt() { return ordinal()+1; }
  public Month succ() { return toMonth(toInt()+1); }
}
class MyDate {
  final int yy /* 0-9999 */, dd /* 1-31 */;
  final Month mm;
  public MyDate(int yy, Month mm, int dd) throws Exception { ... }
  ...
  public static MyDate fromDaynumber(int n) {
    ...
    Month m = Month.Jan;
    int mdays;
    while ((mdays = m.days(y)) < d) {
      d -= mdays;
      m = m.succ();
    }
    return new MyDate(y, m, d);
    ...
  }
  public static Day weekday(int y, Month m, int d) {
    return Day.toDay((toDaynumber(y, m, d)+6) % 7);
  }
  public String toString() { // ISO format such as 2004-07-11
    return String.format("%4d-%02d-%02d", yy, mm.toInt(), dd);
  }
}
```

15   Exceptions, Checked and Unchecked

An *exception* is an object of an exception type: a non-generic subclass of Throwable. It is used to signal and describe an abnormal situation during program execution. The evaluation of an expression or the execution of a statement may throw an exception, either by executing a `throw` statement (section 12.6.5) or by executing a primitive operation, such as array element assignment, that may throw an exception.

A thrown exception may be caught in a dynamically enclosing `try-catch` statement (section 12.6.6). If the exception is not caught, then the entire program execution will be aborted, and information from the exception will be printed on the console. What is printed is determined by the exception's `toString` method.

There are two kinds of exception types: *checked* (those that must be declared in the *throws-clause* of a method or constructor; see section 9.8) and *unchecked* (those that need not be). If the execution of a method or constructor body can throw a checked exception of class E, then class E or a supertype of E must be declared in the *throws-clause* of the method or constructor.

The following table shows part of the exception class hierarchy.

Class	Status	Package
Throwable	checked	java.lang
Error	unchecked	java.lang
AssertionError	unchecked	java.lang
ExceptionInInitializerError	unchecked	java.lang
OutOfMemoryError	unchecked	java.lang
StackOverflowError	unchecked	java.lang
Exception	checked	java.lang
ClassNotFoundException	checked	java.lang
InterruptedException	checked	java.lang
IOException	checked	java.io
CharConversionException	checked	java.io
EOFException	checked	java.io
FileNotFoundException	checked	java.io
InterruptedIOException	checked	java.io
ObjectStreamException	checked	java.io
InvalidClassException	checked	java.io
NotSerializableException	checked	java.io
SyncFailedException	checked	java.io
UnsupportedEncodingException	checked	java.io
UTFDataFormatException	checked	java.io
RuntimeException	unchecked	java.lang
ArithmeticException	unchecked	java.lang
ArrayStoreException	unchecked	java.lang
ClassCastException	unchecked	java.lang
ConcurrentModificationException	unchecked	java.util
IllegalArgumentException	unchecked	java.lang
IllegalFormatException	unchecked	java.util
IllegalMonitorStateException	unchecked	java.lang
IllegalStateException	unchecked	java.lang
IndexOutOfBoundsException	unchecked	java.lang
ArrayIndexOutOfBoundsException	unchecked	java.lang
StringIndexOutOfBoundsException	unchecked	java.lang
NegativeArraySizeException	unchecked	java.util
NoSuchElementException	unchecked	java.util
NullPointerException	unchecked	java.lang
UnsupportedOperationException	unchecked	java.lang

Example 89 Declaring a Checked Exception Class

This is the class of exceptions thrown by method wdayno4 (example 80). Passing a string to the constructor of the superclass (that is, class Exception) causes method toString to append that string to the name of the exception.

```
class WeekdayException extends Exception {
  public WeekdayException(String wday) {
    super("Illegal weekday: " + wday);
  }
}
```

Example 90 All Paths Through a try-catch-finally Statement

To exercise all 18 paths through the try-catch-finally statement (section 12.6.6) in method m in the following program, run it with each of these command line arguments: 101 102 103 201 202 203 301 302 303 411 412 413 421 422 423 431 432 433. The try clause terminates normally on arguments 1*yz*, exits by return on 2*yz*, and throws an exception on 3*yz* and 4*yz*. However, when *z* is 2 or 3, the finally clause determines whether the statement terminates successfully or throws an exception; see below. The catch clause ignores exceptions thrown on 3*yz* but catches those thrown on 4*yz*. The catch clause terminates normally on 411, exits by return on 421, and throws an exception on 431. The finally clause terminates normally on *xy*1 (and so lets the try or catch clause determine how the execution terminates), exits by return on *xy*2 (including on 102 and so on), and throws an exception on *xy*3 (including on 103 and so on).

Exits by break and continue statements are handled similarly to return; a more involved example could be constructed to illustrate their interaction.

```
class TryCatchFinally {
  public static void main(String[] args) throws Exception
  { System.out.println(m(Integer.parseInt(args[0]))); }

  static String m(int a) throws Exception {
    try {
      System.out.print("try ... ");
      if (a/100 == 2) return "returned from try";
      if (a/100 == 3) throw new Exception("thrown by try");
      if (a/100 == 4) throw new RuntimeException("thrown by try");
    } catch (RuntimeException x) {
      System.out.print("catch ... ");
      if (a/10%10 == 2) return "returned from catch";
      if (a/10%10 == 3) throw new Exception("thrown by catch");
    } finally {
      System.out.println("finally");
      if (a%10 == 2) return "returned from finally";
      if (a%10 == 3) throw new Exception("thrown by finally");
    }
    return "terminated normally with " + a;
  }
}
```

16 Threads, Concurrent Execution, and Synchronization

16.1 Threads and Concurrent Execution

The preceding chapters described sequential program execution, in which expressions are evaluated and statements are executed one after the other: they considered only a single thread of execution, where a *thread* is an independent sequential activity. A Java program may execute several threads concurrently, that is, potentially overlapping in time. For instance, one part of a program may continue computing while another part is blocked waiting for input (example 91).

A thread is created and controlled using an object of the Thread class found in the package `java.lang`. A thread executes the method `public void run()` in an object of a class implementing the Runnable interface, also found in package `java.lang`. To every thread (independent sequential activity) there is a unique controlling Thread object, so the two are often thought of as being identical.

One way to create and run a thread is to declare a class U as a subclass of Thread, overwriting its (trivial) run method. Then create an object u of class U and call `u.start()`. This will enable the thread to execute `u.run()` concurrently with other threads (example 91).

Alternatively, declare a class C that implements Runnable, create an object o of that class, create a thread object `u = new Thread(o)` from o, and execute `u.start()`. This will enable the thread to execute `o.run()` concurrently with other threads (example 95).

Threads can communicate with each other via shared state, namely, by using and assigning static fields, non-static fields, array elements, and pipes (section 23.16). By the design of Java, threads cannot use local variables and method parameters for communication.

States and State Transitions of a Thread

A thread is alive if it has been started and has not died. A thread dies by exiting its `run()` method, either by returning or by throwing an exception. A live thread is in one of the states Enabled (ready to run), Running (actually executing), Sleeping (waiting for a timeout), Joining (waiting for another thread to die), Locking (trying to obtain the lock on object o), or Waiting (for notification on object o). The thread state transitions are shown in the following table and the figure on the facing page:

From State	To State	Reason for Transition
Enabled	Running	System schedules thread for execution
Running	Enabled	System preempts thread and schedules another one
	Enabled	Thread executes `yield()`
	Waiting	Thread executes `o.wait()`, releasing lock on o
	Locking	Thread attempts to execute `synchronized (o) { ... }`
	Sleeping	Thread executes `sleep()`
	Joining	Thread executes `u.join()`
	Dead	Thread exited `run()` by returning or by throwing an exception
Sleeping	Enabled	Sleeping period expired
	Enabled	Thread was interrupted; throws InterruptedException when run
Joining	Enabled	Thread u being joined died, or join timed out
	Enabled	Thread was interrupted; throws InterruptedException when run
Waiting	Locking	Another thread executed `o.notify()` or `o.notifyAll()`
	Locking	Wait for lock on o timed out
	Locking	Thread was interrupted; throws InterruptedException when run
Locking	Enabled	Lock on o became available and was given to this thread

Example 91 Multiple Threads

The main program creates a new thread, binds it to u, and starts it. Now two threads are executing concurrently: one executes main, and another executes run. While the main method is blocked waiting for keyboard input, the new thread keeps incrementing i. The new thread executes yield() to make sure that the other thread is allowed to run (when not blocked).

```
class Incrementer extends Thread {
  public int i;
  public void run() {
    for (;;) {                                // Forever
      i++;                                    //   increment i
      yield();
    }
} }

class ThreadDemo {
  public static void main(String[] args) throws IOException {
    Incrementer u = new Incrementer();
    u.start();
    System.out.println("Repeatedly press Enter to get the current value of i:");
    for (;;) {
      System.in.read();                       // Wait for keyboard input
      System.out.println(u.i);
} } }
```

States and State Transitions of a Thread.   A thread's transition from one state to another may be caused by a method call performed by the thread itself (shown in the monospace font), by a method call possibly performed by another thread (shown in the *slanted monospace* font); and by timeouts and other actions.

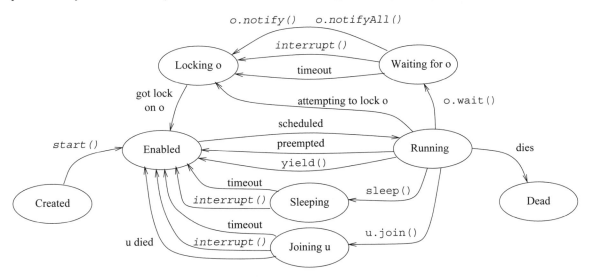

16.2　Locks and the `synchronized` Statement

Concurrent threads are executed independently. Therefore, when multiple concurrent threads access the same fields or array elements, there is considerable risk of creating an inconsistent state (example 93). To avoid this, threads may synchronize the access to shared state, such as objects and arrays. A single *lock* is associated with every object, array, and class. A lock can be held by at most one thread at a time. A thread may explicitly request the lock on an object or array by executing a `synchronized` statement, which has this form:

```
synchronized (expression)
    block-statement
```

The *expression* must have reference type. The *expression* must evaluate to a non-`null` reference o; otherwise a NullPointerException is thrown. After the evaluation of the *expression*, the thread becomes Locking on object o; see the figure on the previous page. When the thread obtains the lock on object o (if ever), the thread becomes Enabled, and may become Running so the *block-statement* is executed. When the *block-statement* terminates or is exited by `return` or `break` or `continue` or by throwing an exception, then the lock on o is released.

A `synchronized` non-static method declaration (section 9.8) is shorthand for a method whose body has the form

```
synchronized (this)
    method-body
```

That is, the thread will execute the method body only when it has obtained the lock on the current object. It will release the lock when it leaves the method body.

A `synchronized` static method declaration (section 9.8) in class C is shorthand for a method whose body has the form

```
synchronized (C.class)
    method-body
```

That is, the thread will execute the method body only when it has obtained the lock on the object C.class, which is the unique object of class Class associated with the class C; see section 24.1. It will hold the lock until it leaves the method body, and release it at that time.

Constructors and initializers cannot be synchronized.

Mutual exclusion is ensured only if *all* threads accessing a shared object lock it before use. For instance, if we add an unsynchronized method `roguetransfer` to a bank object (example 93), we can no longer be sure that a thread calling the synchronized method `transfer` has exclusive access to the bank object: any number of threads could be executing `roguetransfer` at the same time.

A *monitor* is an object whose fields are private and are manipulated only by synchronized methods of the object, so that all field access is subject to synchronization (example 94).

If a thread u needs to wait for some condition to become true, or for a resource to become available, it may temporarily release its lock on object o by calling o.wait(). The thread must hold the lock on object o, otherwise exception IllegalMonitorStateException is thrown. The thread u will be added to the *wait set* of o, that is, the set of threads waiting for notification on object o. This notification must come from another thread that has obtained the lock on o and that executes o.notify() or o.notifyAll(). The notifying thread does not release its lock on o. After being notified, u must obtain the lock on o again before it can proceed. Thus when the call to wait returns, thread u will hold the lock on o just as before the call (example 94).

For detailed rules governing the behavior of unsynchronized Java threads, see chapter 17 of the Java Language Specification [1].

Example 92 Mutual Exclusion

A Printer thread forever prints a dash (-) followed by a slash (/). If we create and run two concurrent printer threads using new Printer().start() and new Printer().start(), then only one of the threads can hold the lock on object mutex at a time, so no other symbols can be printed between (-) and (/) in one iteration of the for loop. Thus the program must print -/-/-/-/-/-/-/ and so on. However, if the synchronization is removed, it may print --//--/-/-//--// and so on. The call Util.pause(200) pauses the thread for 200 ms, whereas Util.pause(100,300) pauses it between 100 and 300 ms. This is done only to make the inherent nondeterminacy of unsynchronized concurrency more easily observable.

```
class Printer extends Thread {
  static Object mutex = new Object();
  public void run() {
    for (;;) {
      synchronized (mutex) {
        System.out.print("-");
        Util.pause(100,300);
        System.out.print("/");
      }
      Util.pause(200);
} } }
```

Example 93 Synchronized Methods in an Object

The Bank object here has two accounts. Money is repeatedly being transferred from one account to the other by clerks. Clearly the total amount of money should remain constant (at 30 euro). This holds true when the transfer method is declared synchronized, because only one clerk can access the accounts at any one time. If the synchronized declaration is removed, the sum will differ from 30 most of the time, because one clerk is likely to overwrite the other's deposits and withdrawals.

```
class Bank {
  private int account1 = 10, account2 = 20;
  synchronized public void transfer(int amount) {
    int new1 = account1 - amount;
    Util.pause(10);
    account1 = new1; account2 = account2 + amount;
    System.out.println("Sum is " + (account1+account2));
} }

class Clerk extends Thread {
  private Bank bank;
  public Clerk(Bank bank) { this.bank = bank; }
  public void run() {
    for (;;) {                                    // Forever
      bank.transfer(Util.random(-10, 10));        //   transfer money
      Util.pause(200, 300);                       //   then take a break
} } }

... Bank bank = new Bank();
... new Clerk(bank).start(); new Clerk(bank).start();
```

16.3   Operations on Threads

The current thread, whose state is Running, may call these methods among others. Further Thread methods are described in the Java class library documentation [3].

- `Thread.yield()` changes the state of the current thread from Running to Enabled, and thereby allows the system to schedule another Enabled thread, if any.

- `Thread.sleep(n)` sleeps for n milliseconds: the current thread becomes Sleeping and after n milliseconds becomes Enabled. May throw InterruptedException if the thread is interrupted while sleeping.

- `Thread.currentThread()` returns the current thread object.

- `Thread.interrupted()` returns and clears the *interrupted status* of the current thread: `true` if there has been no call to `Thread.interrupted()` and no InterruptedException thrown since the last interrupt; otherwise `false`.

Let u be a thread (an object of a subclass of Thread). Then

- `u.start()` changes the state of u to Enabled so that its `run` method will be called when a processor becomes available.

- `u.interrupt()` interrupts the thread u: if u is Running or Enabled or Locking, then its interrupted status is set to `true`. If u is Sleeping or Joining, it will become Enabled, and if it is Waiting, it will become Locking; in these cases u will throw InterruptedException when and if it becomes Running (and the interrupted status is set to `false`).

- `u.isInterrupted()` returns the interrupted status of u (and does not clear it).

- `u.join()` waits for thread u to die; may throw InterruptedException if the current thread is interrupted while waiting.

- `u.join(n)` works as `u.join()` but times out and returns after at most n milliseconds. There is no indication whether the call returned because of a timeout or because u died.

16.4   Operations on Locked Objects

A thread that holds the lock on an object o may call the following methods, inherited by o from class Object.

- `o.wait()` releases the lock on o, changes its own state to Waiting, and adds itself to the set of threads waiting for notification on o. When notified (if ever), the thread must obtain the lock on o, so when the call to `wait` returns, it again holds the lock on o. May throw InterruptedException if the thread is interrupted while waiting.

- `o.wait(n)` works like `o.wait()` except that the thread will change state to Locking after n milliseconds regardless of whether there has been a notification on o. There is no indication whether the state change was caused by a timeout or because of a notification.

- `o.notify()` chooses an arbitrary thread among the threads waiting for notification on o (if any) and changes its state to Locking. The chosen thread cannot actually obtain the lock on o until the current thread has released it.

- `o.notifyAll()` works like `o.notify()`, except that it changes the state to Locking for *all* threads waiting for notification on o.

Example 94 Producers and Consumers Communicating via a Monitor

A Buffer has room for one integer, and has a method `put` for storing into the buffer (if empty) and a method `get` for reading from the buffer (if non-empty); it is a monitor (section 16.2). A thread calling `get` must obtain the lock on the buffer. If it finds that the buffer is empty, it calls `wait` to (release the lock and) wait until something has been put into the buffer. If another thread calls `put` and thus `notifyAll`, then the getting thread will start competing for the buffer lock again, and if it gets it, will continue executing. Here we have used a `synchronized` statement in the method body (instead of making the method `synchronized`) to emphasize that synchronization, `wait`, and `notifyAll` all work on the same buffer object `this`.

```
class Buffer {
  private int contents;
  private boolean empty = true;
  public int get() {
    synchronized (this) {
      while (empty)
        try { this.wait(); } catch (InterruptedException x) {};
      empty = true;
      this.notifyAll();
      return contents;
  } }
  public void put(int v) {
    synchronized (this) {
      while (!empty)
        try { this.wait(); } catch (InterruptedException x) {};
      empty = false;
      contents = v;
      this.notifyAll();
  } }
}
```

Example 95 Graphic Animation Using the Runnable Interface

Class AnimatedCanvas here is a subclass of Canvas and so cannot be a subclass of Thread also. Instead it declares a `run` method and implements the Runnable interface. The constructor creates a Thread object u from the AnimatedCanvas object `this` and then starts the thread. The new thread executes the `run` method, which repeatedly sleeps and repaints, thus creating an animation.

```
class AnimatedCanvas extends Canvas implements Runnable {
  AnimatedCanvas() { Thread u = new Thread(this); u.start(); }

  public void run() {                         // From interface Runnable
    for (;;) { // Forever sleep and repaint
      try { Thread.sleep(100); } catch (InterruptedException e) { }
      ...
      repaint();
    }
  }

  public void paint(Graphics g) { ... }       // From class Canvas
  ...
}
```

17 Compilation, Source Files, Class Names, and Class Files

A *Java program* consists of one or more *source files* (with file name suffix .java). A source file may contain one or more class or interface declarations. A source file can contain at most one declaration of a top-level public class or interface, which must then have the same name as the file (minus the file name suffix). A source file myprog.java is compiled to Java class files (with file name suffix .class) by a Java compiler:

```
javac myprog.java
```

This creates one class file for each class or interface declared in the source file myprog.java. A class or interface C declared in a top-level declaration produces a class file called C.class. A nested class or interface D declared inside class C produces a class file called C$D.class. A local class D declared inside a method in class C produces a class file called C1D.class or similar.

A Java class C that declares the method public static void main(String[] args) can be executed using the Java run-time system java by typing a command line of the form

```
java C arg1 arg2 ...
```

This will execute the body of method main with the command line arguments *arg*1, *arg*2, ... bound to the array elements args[0], args[1], ... inside the method main (examples 9 and 100).

18 Packages and Jar Files

Java source files may be organized in *packages*. Every source file in package p must begin with the declaration

```
package p;
```

and must be stored in a subdirectory called p. A class declared in a source file with no package declaration belongs to the anonymous *default package*. A source file not belonging to package p may refer to class C from package p by using the qualified name p.C, in which the class name C is prefixed by the package name. To avoid using the package name prefix, the source file may begin with an import declaration (possibly following a package declaration) of one of three forms:

```
import p.C;
import p.*;
import static p.C.*;
```

The first form allows C to be used unqualified, without the package name, and the second one allows all accessible classes and interfaces in package p to be used unqualified. The third form allows all static members of class C to be used unqualified; see example 165. The Java class library package java.lang is implicitly imported, so all java.lang classes can be used unqualified in Java source files. Note that java.lang is a composite package name, so class java.lang.String is declared in file java/lang/String.java.

The files in p and its subdirectories can be collected in a *jar file* by executing jar vcf p.jar p on the command line. The packages in the resulting jar file p.jar can be made available to other Java programs by moving the file to the directory /usr/java/jdk1.5.0/jre/lib/ext or similar under Unix, or to the directory c:\jdk1.5\jre\lib\ext or similar under MS Windows. The jar file may contain more than one package; it need only contain class files (not source files); and its name is not significant.

Example 96 The Vessel Hierarchy as a Package

The package vessel here contains part of the vessel hierarchy (example 27). The fields in classes Tank and Barrel are final, so they cannot be modified after object creation. They are protected, so they are accessible in subclasses declared outside the vessel package, as shown in file Usevessels.java, which is in the anonymous default package, not in the vessel package.

The file vessel/Vessel.java

```
package vessel;
public abstract class Vessel {
  private double contents;
  public abstract double capacity();
  public final void fill(double amount)
  { contents = Math.min(contents + amount, capacity()); }
  public final double getContents() { return contents; }
}
```

The file vessel/Tank.java

```
package vessel;
public class Tank extends Vessel {
  protected final double length, width, height;
  public Tank(double l, double w, double h) { length = l; width = w; height = h; }
  public double capacity() { return length * width * height; }
  public String toString()
  { return "tank (l,w,h) = (" + length + ", " + width + ", " + height + ")"; }
}
```

The file vessel/Barrel.java

```
package vessel;
public class Barrel extends Vessel {
  protected final double radius, height;
  public Barrel(double r, double h) { radius = r; height = h; }
  public double capacity() { return height * Math.PI * radius * radius; }
  public String toString() { return "barrel (r, h) = (" + radius + ", " + height + ")"; }
}
```

The file Usevessels.java

Subclass Cube of class Tank may access the field length because that field is declared protected in Tank above. The main method is unmodified from example 28.

```
import vessel.*;
class Cube extends Tank {
  public Cube(double side) { super(side, side, side); }
  public String toString() { return "cube (s) = (" + length + ")"; }
}
class Usevessels {
    public static void main(String[] args) { ... }
}
```

19   Mathematical Functions

Class Math provides static methods to compute standard mathematical functions. Floating-point numbers (double and float) include positive and negative infinities as well as non-numbers (NaN), following the IEEE754 standard [8]. There is also a distinction between positive zero and negative zero, ignored here.

The Math methods return non-numbers (NaN) when applied to illegal arguments, and return infinities in case of overflow; they do not throw exceptions. Also, the methods return NaN when applied to NaN arguments, except where noted, and behave sensibly when applied to positive or negative infinities.

Angles are given and returned in radians, not degrees. Methods that round to nearest integer will round to the nearest even integer in case of a tie. The methods abs, min, and max are overloaded on float, int, and long arguments also. There are also hyperbolic trigonometric functions cosh, sinh and tanh.

- static double E is the constant $e \approx 2.71828$, the base of the natural logarithm.
- static double PI is the constant $\pi \approx 3.14159$, the circumference of a circle with diameter 1.
- static double abs(double x) is the absolute value: x if x>=0, and -x if x<0.
- static double acos(double x) is the arc cosine of x, in the range $[0, \pi]$, for -1<=x<=1.
- static double asin(double x) is the arc sine of x, in the range $[-\pi/2, \pi/2]$, for -1<=x<=1.
- static double atan(double x) is the arc tangent of x, in the range $[-\pi/2, \pi/2]$.
- static double atan2(double y, double x) is the arc tangent of y/x in the quadrant of the point (x, y), in the range $]-\pi, \pi]$. When x is 0, the result is $\pi/2$ with the same sign as y.
- static double ceil(double x) is the smallest integral double value >=x.
- static double cbrt(double x) is the cube root x; for negative x, cbrt(x) equals -cbrt(-x).
- static double cos(double x) is the cosine of x, in the range $[-1, 1]$.
- static double exp(double x) is the exponential of x, that is, e to the power x.
- static double floor(double x) is the largest integral double value <=x.
- static double IEEEremainder(double x, double y) is the remainder of x/y, that is, x-y*n, where n is the mathematical integer closest to x/y.
- static double log(double x) is the natural logarithm (to base e) of x, for x>=0.
- static double log10(double x) is the logarithm (to base 10) of x, for x>=0.
- static double max(double x, double y) is the greatest of x and y.
- static double min(double x, double y) is the smallest of x and y.
- static double pow(double x, double y) is x to the power y, that is, x^y. If y is 0, then the result is 1.0. If y is 1, then the result is x. If x<0 and y is not integral, then the result is NaN.
- static double random() returns a uniformly distributed pseudo-random number in $[0, 1[$.
- static double rint(double x) is the integral double value that is closest to x.
- static long round(double x) is the long value that is closest to x.
- static int round(float x) is the int value that is closest to x.
- static double sin(double x) is the sine of x radians.
- static double signum(double x) is -1.0 or 0.0 or $+1.0$ according as x is negative, zero or positive.
- static double sqrt(double x) is the positive square root of x, for x>=0.
- static double tan(double x) is the tangent of x radians.
- static double toDegrees(double r) is the number of degrees corresponding to r radians.
- static double toRadians(double d) is the number of radians corresponding to d degrees.

Example 97 Floating-Point Factorial
This method computes the factorial function $n! = 1 \cdot 2 \cdot 3 \cdots (n-1) \cdot n$ using logarithms.

```
static double fact(int n) {
  double res = 0.0;
  for (int i=1; i<=n; i++)
    res += Math.log(i);
  return Math.exp(res);
}
```

Example 98 Generating Gaussian Pseudo-Random Numbers
This example uses the Box-Muller transformation to generate N Gaussian, or normally distributed, pseudo-random numbers with mean 0 and standard deviation 1.

```
for (int i=0; i<N; i+=2) {
  double x1 = Math.random(), x2 = Math.random();
  print(Math.sqrt(-2 * Math.log(x1)) * Math.cos(2 * Math.PI * x2));
  print(Math.sqrt(-2 * Math.log(x1)) * Math.sin(2 * Math.PI * x2));
}
```

Example 99 Mathematical Functions: Infinities, NaNs, and Special Cases

```
print("Illegal arguments, NaN results:");
print(Math.sqrt(-1));              // NaN
print(Math.log(-1));               // NaN
print(Math.pow(-1, 2.5));          // NaN
print(Math.acos(1.1));             // NaN
print("Infinite results:");
print(Math.log(0));                // -Infinity
print(Math.pow(0, -1));            // Infinity
print(Math.exp(1000.0));           // Infinity (overflow)
print("Infinite arguments:");
double infinity = Double.POSITIVE_INFINITY;
print(Math.sqrt(infinity));        // Infinity
print(Math.log(infinity));         // Infinity
print(Math.exp(-infinity));        // 0.0
print("NaN arguments and special cases:");
double nan = Math.log(-1);
print(Math.sqrt(nan));             // NaN
print(Math.pow(nan, 0));           // 1.0 (special case)
print(Math.pow(0, 0));             // 1.0 (special case)
print(Math.round(nan));            // 0   (special case)
print(Math.round(1E50));           // 9223372036854775807 (Long.MAX_VALUE)
// For all (x, y) except (0.0, 0.0):
// sign(cos(atan2(y, x))) == sign(x) && sign(sin(atan2(y, x))) == sign(y)
for (double x=-100; x<=100; x+=0.125) {
  for (double y=-100; y<=100; y+=0.125) {
    double r = Math.atan2(y, x);
    if (!(sign(Math.cos(r))==sign(x) && sign(Math.sin(r))==sign(y)))
      print("x = " + x + "; y = " + y);
  }
}
```

20   String Builders and String Buffers

A String object s1, once created, cannot be modified. Using s1 + s2 one can append another string s2 to s1, but that creates a new string object, copying all the characters from s1 and s2; there is no way to extend s1 itself by appending more characters to it. Thus to concatenate n strings each of length k by repeated string concatenation (+), we copy $k + 2k + 3k + \cdots + nk = kn(n+1)/2$ characters, and the time required to do this is proportional to kn^2, which grows rapidly as n grows.

String builders, which are objects of the predefined class java.lang.StringBuilder, provide extensible and modifiable strings. Characters can be appended to a string builder without copying those characters already in the string builder; the string builder is automatically and efficiently extended as needed. To concatenate n strings each of length k using a string builder requires only time proportional to kn, considerably faster than kn^2 for large n. Thus to gradually build a string, use a string builder. This is needed only for repeated concatenation in a loop, as in example 9. The expression s1 + $\cdots$ + sn is efficient; it actually means new StringBuilder().append(s1).$\cdots$.append(sn).toString().

Let sb be a StringBuilder, s a String, and v an expression of any type. Then

- new StringBuilder() creates a new empty string builder.

- sb.append(v) appends the string representation of the value v to the string builder, converting v by String.valueOf(v), see chapter 7. Extends sb as needed. Returns sb.

- sb.charAt(int i) returns character number i (counting from zero) in the string builder. Throws StringIndexOutOfBoundsException if i<0 or i>=sb.length().

- sb.delete(from, to) deletes the characters with index from..(to-1) from the string builder, reducing its length by to-from characters. Throws StringIndexOutOfBoundsException if from<0 or from>to or to>sb.length(). Returns sb.

- sb.insert(from, v) inserts the string representation of v obtained by String.valueOf(v) into the string builder, starting at position from, extending sb as needed. Returns sb. Throws StringIndexOutOfBoundsException if from<0 or from>sb.length().

- sb.length() of type int is the length of sb, that is, the number of characters currently in sb.

- sb.replace(from, to, s) replaces the characters with index from..(to-1) in the string builder by the string s, extending sb if needed. Throws StringIndexOutOfBoundsException if from<0 or from>to or from>sb.length(). Returns sb.

- sb.reverse() reverses the character sequence in the string builder. Returns sb.

- sb.setCharAt(i, c) sets the character at index i to c. Throws StringIndexOutOfBoundsException if i<0 or i>=sb.length().

- sb.toString() of type String is a new string containing the characters currently in sb.

- Method append is fast, but delete, insert, and replace may be slow when they need to move large parts of the string builder — when both from and to are much smaller than length().

A StringBuffer has the same methods as a StringBuilder, but is thread-safe: several concurrent threads (chapter 16) can modify the same string buffer without making its internal state inconsistent. More StringBuilder and StringBuffer methods are described in the Java class library documentation [3].

Example 100 Efficiently Concatenating All Command Line Arguments

When there are many (more than 50) command line arguments, this is much faster than example 9.

```
public static void main(String[] args) {
  StringBuilder res = new StringBuilder();
  for (int i=0; i<args.length; i++)
    res.append(args[i]);
  System.out.println(res.toString());
}
```

Example 101 Replacing Occurrences of a Character by a String

To replace occurrences of character c1 with the string s2 in string s, it is best to use a string builder for the result, since the size of the resulting string is not known in advance. This works well also when replacing a character c1 with another character c2, but in that case the length of the result is known in advance (it equals the length of s) and one can use a character array instead (example 21). Solving this problem by repeated string concatenation (using res += s2) would be very slow.

```
static String replaceCharString(String s, char c1, String s2) {
  StringBuilder res = new StringBuilder();
  for (int i=0; i<s.length(); i++)
    if (s.charAt(i) == c1)
      res.append(s2);
    else
      res.append(s.charAt(i));
  return res.toString();
}
```

Example 102 Inefficiently Replacing Occurrences of a Character by a String

The problem from example 101 can also be solved by destructively modifying a string builder with replace. However, repeatedly using replace is inefficient: for a string of 200,000 random characters this method is approximately 100 times slower than the one in example 101.

```
static void replaceCharString(StringBuilder sb, char c1, String s2) {
  int i = 0;                                // Inefficient
  while (i < sb.length()) {                 // Inefficient
    if (sb.charAt(i) == c1) {               // Inefficient
      sb.replace(i, i+1, s2);               // Inefficient
      i += s2.length();                     // Inefficient
    } else                                  // Inefficient
      i += 1;                               // Inefficient
} }                                         // Inefficient
```

Example 103 Padding a String to a Given Width

A string s may be padded with spaces to give it a certain minimum width, to align data into columns when using a fixed-pitch font. But this is supported also by the string formatting facilities; see section 7.1.

```
static String padLeft(String s, int width) {
  StringBuilder res = new StringBuilder();
  for (int i=width-s.length(); i>0; i--)
    res.append(' ');
  return res.append(s).toString();
}
```

21   Generic Types and Methods (Java 5.0)

Generic types and methods provide a way to strengthen type checking at compile-time while at the same time making programs more expressive, reusable and readable. The ability to have generic types and methods is also known as parametric polymorphism.

21.1   Generics: Safety, Generality, and Efficiency

The original Java language did not support generic types and methods. Therefore a library for manipulating arbitrary kinds of values would have to cast those values to type Object. For instance, we might use an ArrayList `cool` to hold Person objects, but the `add` and `get` methods of the `cool` arraylist would have to accept and return values of type Object. This works, but has several negative consequences that can be avoided by using generic types; see examples 104 and 105.

21.2   Generic Types, Type Parameters, and Type Instances

A *generic class* declaration class `C<T1,...,Tn>` { ... } has one or more *type parameters* `T1,...,Tn`. The body of the declaration is an ordinary class body (section 9.1) in which the type parameters `Ti` can be used almost as if they were ordinary types; see section 21.6. A generic class is also called a parametrized class.

A generic class `C<T1>` is not itself a class. Rather, it is a mechanism or template from which classes such as C<Integer> or C<String> or even C<C<String>>, and so on, can be generated, by replacing the type parameter `T1` by a type expression `t1`, such as Integer or String or C<String>. The resulting classes are called *type instances*. The type `t1` used to replace the type parameter `T1` can be any reference type expression: a class, an array type, an interface, or it can itself be a type instance. However, it cannot be a primitive type such as int, nor the pseudo-type void (which can be used only to indicate that a method has no return value).

Generic interfaces (section 21.7) can be declared also, and type instances can be created from them. Again, a generic interface is not an interface, but a type instance of a generic interface is an interface.

Generic methods (section 21.8) can be declared by specifying type parameters on the method declaration in addition to any type parameters specified on the enclosing class or interface type.

Section 21.11 compares the implementation of Java generic types and methods with C++ templates and C# 2.0 generic types and methods.

21.3   How Can Type Instances Be Used?

A type instance such as C<Integer> can be used almost anywhere an ordinary reference type can be used: as the type of a field, variable, parameter or return type; as the element type in an array type in the same contexts; as a constructor name new `C<T>(...)`; and so on. However, there are the following restrictions:

- One can use a type instance in cast expression such as `(C<Integer>)e` but such a cast is sometimes reported by the compiler to be unchecked (see section 21.6).

- One cannot use a type instance in an instance test expression such as `(e instanceof C<Integer>)`.

- One cannot use a type instance as the element type of an array in an array creation expression such as new `C<Integer>[5]`. But new `ArrayList<C<Integer>>()` is legal; see section 21.11.

Example 104 Using Non-Generic ArrayList: Run-Time Type Checks and Wrapping of Values

The java.util.ArrayList `cool` should hold only Person objects, but without generic types, the compiler cannot check that only Person objects are added to `cool`. Hence at run-time the program must check and cast objects when extracting them from the list. These checks take time, and may fail. The Java compiler can only warn that maybe the add operations are suspicious:

```
ArrayList cool = new ArrayList();
cool.add(new Person("Kristen"));
cool.add(new Person("Bjarne"));
cool.add(new Exception("Larry"));     // Wrong, but no compiletime check
cool.add(new Person("Anders"));
Person p = (Person)(cool.get(2));     // Compiles OK, but fails at runtime
```

Example 105 Using Generic ArrayList: Compile-Time Type Checks

With generic types, `cool` can be declared to have type java.util.ArrayList<Person>, the compiler can check that only Person objects are passed to the `cool.add` method, and therefore the array list `cool` can contain only Person objects. Thus generic types make the programmer's intention clear in the source code and improve our trust in the program.

However, Java 5.0 generic types do not improve efficiency: the cast to class Person after `cool.get(2)` is still performed at run-time, but it does not appear explicitly in the source code.

```
ArrayList<Person> cool = new ArrayList<Person>();
cool.add(new Person("Kristen"));
cool.add(new Person("Bjarne"));
cool.add(new Exception("Larry"));     // Wrong, detected at compile-time
cool.add(new Person("Anders"));
Person p = cool.get(2);               // No explicit cast or check needed
```

Example 106 A Generic Class Type for Pairs

A pair of two values of type T and U can be represented by a generic class Pair<T,U>. The generic class has read-only fields for holding the components, and a constructor for creating pairs.

```
class Pair<T,U> {
  public final T fst;
  public final U snd;
  public Pair(T fst, U snd) {
    this.fst = fst;
    this.snd = snd;
  }
}
...
Pair<String,Integer> p1 = new Pair<String,Integer>("Niels", 1947);
Pair<Double,Integer> p2 = new Pair<Double,Integer>(2.718, 1);
Pair<Date,String> p3 = new Pair<Date,String>(new Date(), "now");
```

21.4 Generic Classes

A declaration of a *generic class* C<T1,...,Tn> may have this form:

> *class-modifiers* class C<T1,...,Tn> *class-base-clause*
> *class-body*

The T1,...,Tn are *type parameters*. The *class-modifiers*, *class-body* and *class-base-clause* are as for a non-generic class declaration (section 9.1).

In addition, each type parameter Ti may have constraints c_1, c_2, ..., c_n, in which case its entry in the parameter list is written Ti extends c_1 & c_2 & ... & c_n instead of just Ti; see section 21.5.

The type parameters T1,...,Tn may be used wherever a type is expected in the *class-base-clause* and in non-static members of the *class-body*, and so may the type parameters of any enclosing generic class, if the present class is a non-static member class. See section 21.6 for details.

A generic class C<T1,...,Tn> in itself is not a class. However, each *type instance* C<t1,...,tn> is a class, just like a class declared by replacing each type parameter Ti with the corresponding type ti in the *class-body*. A type ti that is substituted for a type parameter Ti in a type instance can be any reference type: a class, an array type, an interface, an enum type, or it can itself be a type instance. However, it cannot be a primitive type nor the pseudo-type void; the void pseudo-type can be used only to indicate that a method has no return value.

All type instances of a generic class C<T1,...,Tn> are represented by the same *raw type* C at run-time. All type instances of a generic class C<T1,...,Tn> share the same static fields (if any) declared in the *class-body*. As a consequence, the type parameters of the class cannot be used in any static members.

A type instance C<t1,...,tn> is accessible when all its parts are accessible. Thus if the generic class C<T1,...,Tn> or any of the type arguments t1,...,tn is private, then the type instance is private also.

A scope can have only one class, generic or not, with the same name C, regardless of its number of type parameters.

A generic class declaration is illegal if there are types t1,...,tn such that the type instance C<t1,...,tn> would contain two or more method declarations with the same signature.

The usual conversion rules hold for generic classes and generic interfaces. When generic class C<T1> is declared to be a subclass of generic class B<T1> or is declared to implement interface I<T1>, then the type instance C<t1> is a subtype of the type instances B<t1> and I<t1>: an expression of type C<t1> can be used wherever a value of type B<t1> or I<t1> is expected.

However, generic classes and interfaces are invariant in their type parameters. Hence even if t11 is a subtype of t12, the type instance C<t11> is not a subtype of the type instance C<t12>. For example, LinkedList<String> is not a subtype of LinkedList<Object>. If it were, one could create a LinkedList<String>, cast it to LinkedList<Object>, store an Object into it, and rather unexpectedly get an Object back out of the original LinkedList<String>.

Example 107 A Generic Class for Logging

Generic class Log<T> implements a simple log that stores the last few objects of type T written to it. To create a Log<T> one must provide an array of type `T[]` to hold the log entries. Method `add` accepts new log entries of type T and method `getLast` returns the latest log entry. Method `getAll` returns an ArrayList<T> of all the available log entries; it cannot create and return an array of type `T[]`, see section 21.11.

```
class Log<T> {
  private final int size;
  private static int instanceCount = 0;
  private int count = 0;
  private T[] log;
  public Log(T[] log) { this.log = log; this.size = log.length; instanceCount++; }
  public void add(T msg) { log[count++ % size] = msg; }
  public T getLast() {
    return count==0 ? null : log[(count-1)%size];
  }
  public void setLast(T value) { ... }
  public ArrayList<T> getAll() { ... }
}
...
Log<Date> log2 = new Log<Date>(new Date[5]);
log2.add(new Date());                                   // now
```

Example 108 A Generic Linked List Class

An object of generic class MyLinkedList<T> is a linked list whose elements have type T; it implements interface MyList<T> (example 112). The generic class declaration has a static nested class Node<U>; two constructors, one of which takes a variable number of arguments of type T; methods that take arguments of type T, an `equals` method that casts its argument to MyList<T> (by an unchecked cast), and a method that returns an Iterator<T>. See also example 117.

```
class MyLinkedList<T> implements MyList<T> {
  protected int size;              // Number of elements in the list
  protected Node<T> first, last;   // Invariant: first==null iff last==null
  protected static class Node<U> {  // Static nested generic class
    public Node<U> prev, next;
    public U item;
    ...
  }
  public MyLinkedList() { first = last = null; size = 0; }
  public MyLinkedList(T... arr) { ... }        // Variable-arity constructor
  public void add(T item) { insert(size, item); }
  public void insert(int i, T item) { ... }
  public void removeAt(int i) { ... }
  public boolean equals(Object that) {
    return equals((MyList<T>)that);            // Unchecked cast
  }
  public boolean equals(MyList<T> that) { ... }
  public Iterator<T> iterator() { ... }
  ...
}
```

21.5 Constraints on Type Parameters

A type parameter of a generic class C<T1, ..., Tn> may have type parameter constraints. The constraints on a type parameter are given in-line in the type parameter list by a *constraint-clause* of this form:

> Ti extends c_1 & c_2 & ... & c_n

In the constraint clause, Ti is one of the type parameters T1, ..., Tn, each c_j is a *constraint* on Ti, and $n \geq 1$. A *constraint* c must be a type expression: an interface or a non-final class type or one of the preceding type parameters Tj where $1 \leq j \leq$ i-1.

The type expression may be a type instance and may involve any of the type parameters T1, ..., Tn. An array type cannot be used as a constraint.

Only the first constraint c_1 can be a class type or a type parameter Tj; the following ones must be interfaces. If the first constraint is a type parameter Tj, then that must be the only constraint.

Forwards references to type parameters are permitted in a constraint that is a generic type instance such as D<T2>, as in class C<T1 extends D<T2>, T2> { ... }, but they are not permitted when the constraint is a naked type parameter such as T2, as in class C<T1 extends T2, T2> { ... }. This ensures that there can be no constraint cycles.

The types t1, ..., tn used when creating a generic type instance C<t1, ..., tn> must satisfy the *constraints*: if type parameter Ti is replaced by type ti throughout its *constraint-clause*, where the resulting constraint is ti extends c_1 & c_2 & ... & c_n, it must hold that ti is a subtype of c_1 and of c_2 and so on up to c_n.

21.6 How Can Type Parameters Be Used?

Within the body { ... } of a generic class class C<T1, ..., Tn> { ... } or generic interface, a type parameter Ti may be used almost as if it were a public type.

- One can use type parameter Ti to specify the supertype and the implemented interfaces of the generic class or generic interface.

- One can use type parameter Ti in the return type, variable types and parameter types of non-static methods and their local inner classes, and in the type and initializer of non-static fields and non-static constructors. In these contexts, Ti can be used in type instances C1<..., Ti, ...> of generic types C1.

- One can use type parameter Ti for the same purposes in non-static member classes, but not in static member classes nor in member interfaces.

- One can use (Ti) e for type casts, but such casts are sometimes reported by the compiler to be unchecked. See examples 111 and 119.

- One cannot use new Ti[10] to create a new array whose element type is Ti, see example 120; one cannot use (o instanceof Ti) to test whether o is an instance of Ti; one cannot use Ti.class to obtain the canonical object representing the type Ti; one cannot use new Ti() to create an instance of Ti; and one cannot call static methods on a type parameter Ti, as in Ti.m(), or otherwise refer to the static members of a type parameter.

Example 109 Type Parameter Constraints

Interface Printable describes a method `print` that will print an object on a PrintWriter. The generic PrintableLinkedList<T> can implement Printable provided the list elements (of type T) do.

```
class PrintableMyLinkedList<T extends Printable>
  extends MyLinkedList<T> implements Printable
{
  public void print(PrintWriter fs) {
    for (T x : this)
      x.print(fs);
  }
}
interface Printable { void print(PrintWriter fs); }
```

Example 110 Constraints Involving Type Parameters

The elements of a type T are *mutually comparable* if any T-value x can be compared to any T-value y using `x.compareTo(y)`. This is the case if type T implements Comparable<T>; see section 22.8. The requirement that T implements Comparable<T> is expressible by the constraint `T extends Comparable<T>`.

Type ComparablePair<T,U> is a type of ordered pairs of (T,U)-values. For (T,U)-pairs to support comparison, both T and U must support comparison, so constraints are required on both T and U.

```
class ComparablePair<T extends Comparable<T>, U extends Comparable<U>>
  implements Comparable<ComparablePair<T,U>>
{
  public final T fst;
  public final U snd;
  public ComparablePair(T fst, U snd) { this.fst = fst; this.snd = snd; }
  public int compareTo(ComparablePair<T,U> that) {    // Lexicographic ordering
    int firstCmp = this.fst.compareTo(that.fst);
    return firstCmp != 0 ? firstCmp : this.snd.compareTo(that.snd);
  }
}
```

Example 111 Unchecked Cast to Type Parameter

Generic class Hold<T> can hold one element of type T. The set-method accepts an Object x and casts it to T before storing it, so the get-method should return an object of type T. But the "unchecked" cast `(T)x` in `set` is actually not performed, so `set` never throws ClassCastException. However, any attempt to use a non-T result of `get` will throw ClassCastException. The corresponding type-erased code in example 119 shows why.

```
class Hold<T> {
  private T contents;
  public void set(Object x) { contents = (T)x; }    // Unchecked cast
  public T get() { return contents; }
}
...
Hold<Integer> h = new Hold<Integer>();
h.set("foo");                         // Succeeds at run-time
h.get();                              // Succeeds at run-time
// String s = h.get();                // Illegal, rejected by compiler
Integer i = h.get();                  // Legal, but fails at run-time
```

21.7   Generic Interfaces

A declaration of a *generic interface* I<T1, . . . , Tn> has this form:

> *interface-modifiers* interface I<T1, . . . , Tn> *extends-clause*
>   *interface-body*

The T1, . . . , Tn are type parameters as for generic classes (section 21.4), and the *interface-modifiers, extends-clause* and *interface-body* are as for non-generic interfaces (section 13.1). Each type parameter Ti may have type parameter constraints just as for a generic class; see section 21.5.

A type instance of the generic interface has form I<t1, . . . , tn> where the t1, . . . , tn are types. The types t1, . . . , tn must satisfy the parameter constraints, if any, on the generic interface I<T1, . . . , Tn> as described in section 21.5.

A generic interface is a subinterface of the interfaces mentioned in its *extends-clause*. Like a generic class, a generic interface is not covariant in its type parameters. That is, I<String> is not a subtype of I<Object> although String is a subtype of Object.

Example 112 A Generic List Interface
The generic interface MyList<T> extends the Iterable<T> interface (section 22.7) with methods to add and remove list elements, methods to get and set the element at a particular position, and with a generic method <U> map that takes an argument of type Mapper<T,U> (example 113), and builds a list of type MyList<U>. Note that the generic method <U> map has an additional type parameter U.

```
interface MyList<T> extends Iterable<T> {
  int getCount();                    // Number of elements
  T get(int i);                      // Get element at index i
  void set(int i, T item);           // Set element at index i
  void add(T item);                  // Add element at end
  void insert(int i, T item);        // Insert element at index i
  void removeAt(int i);              // Remove element at index i
  <U> MyList<U> map(Mapper<T,U> f);  // Map f over all elements
}
```

Example 113 A Generic Interface Representing a Function
The generic interface Mapper<A,R> describes a single method `call` that takes an argument of type A and returns a result of type R. In other words, Mapper<A,R> is the type of functions from type A to type R, and objects of type Mapper<A,R> can be used where one would use delegates in C# or functions as values in functional languages. This generic interface is used in examples 112 and 117.

```
interface Mapper<A,R> {
  R call(A x);
}
```

Example 114 Subtype Relations between Generic Classes and Interfaces
A LabelPoint<L> is a point with a label of type T; such a point is Movable. A ColorLabelPoint<L,C> is a LabelPoint<L> that additionally has a 'color' of type C. Hence the type instance LabelPoint<String> is a subtype of Movable, and both ColorLabelPoint<String,Integer> and ColorLabelPoint<String,Color> are subtypes of LabelPoint<String> and Movable.

```
interface Movable { void move(int dx, int dy); }
class LabelPoint<L> implements Movable {
  protected int x, y;
  private L lab;
  public LabelPoint(int x, int y, L lab) { this.x = x; this.y = y; this.lab = lab; }
  public void move(int dx, int dy) { x += dx; y += dy; }
}
class ColorLabelPoint<L, C> extends LabelPoint<L> {
  private C c;
  public ColorLabelPoint(int x, int y, L lab, C c) { super(x, y, lab); this.c = c; }
}
```

21.8 Generic Methods

A generic method is a method that takes one or more type parameters. A generic method may be declared inside a generic or non-generic class or interface.

A declaration of a generic method m<T1,...,Tn> has this form:

> *method-modifiers* <T1,...,Tn> *returntype* m (*formal-list*)
> *method-body*

The *method-modifiers*, *returntype*, and *formal-list* are as for non-generic methods (section 9.8). The main syntactic difference is that a generic method has a list of type parameters T1,...,Tn before its *returntype*. Each type parameter Ti may have type parameter constraints just as for a generic class; see section 21.5.

The type parameters T1,...,Tn may be used as types in the *returntype*, *formal-list* and *method-body*; as may the type parameters of any enclosing generic class if the method is non-static. A type parameter Ti of a generic method may have the same name as a type parameter of an enclosing generic class.

Generic methods of the same name m are not distinguished by their number of generic type parameters, and a generic method is not distinguished from a non-generic method of the same name. For example, these three methods

```
void m() { ... }
<T> void m() { ... }
<T,U> void m() { ... }
```

are not considered distinct, and at most one of them can be declared in a given scope.

If a generic method overrides a generic method declared in a superclass or implements a generic method described in an interface, then it must have the same parameter constraints as those methods. The names of the type parameters are not significant, only their ordinal positions in the type parameter list T1,...,Tn.

A call of a generic method can be written without type arguments as in o.m(...), or with explicit generic type arguments as in o.<t1,...,tn>m(...). In the former case, the compiler will attempt to infer the appropriate type arguments t1,...,tn automatically. Type parameter constraints are not taken into account during such inference, but must be satisfied by the resulting type arguments t1,...,tn when inference is successful.

Explicit generic type arguments can be given in four of the syntactic forms of method call (section 11.12):

> o.<t1,...,tn>m(*actual-list*)
> super.<t1,...,tn>m(*actual-list*)
> C.<t1,...,tn>m(*actual-list*)
> C.super.<t1,...,tn>m(*actual-list*)

Note that to give type arguments to a static method m in class C, one must explicitly prefix the method call with the class name, as in C.<t1,...,tn>m(...). Similarly, to give type arguments to an instance method in the current object, one must explicitly prefix the method call with the current object reference, as in this.<t1,...,tn>m(...). In any case, either none or all type arguments must be given.

Example 115 A Generic Quicksort Method Using a Comparator Object
This sorts an array of type `T[]` where `T` is a type parameter. The `Comparator<T>` parameter determines the element ordering; see section 22.8. Also shown are two calls of the method (in class GenericFunQuicksort), without and with explicit type argument. Class IntegerComparator is from example 132.

```
private static <T> void qsort(T[] arr, Comparator<T> cmp, int a, int b) {
  if (a < b) {
    int i = a, j = b;
    T x = arr[(i+j) / 2];
    do {
      while (cmp.compare(arr[i], x) < 0) i++;
      while (cmp.compare(x, arr[j]) < 0) j--;
      if (i <= j) {
        T tmp = arr[i]; arr[i] = arr[j]; arr[j] = tmp;
        i++; j--;
      }
    } while (i <= j);
    qsort(arr, cmp, a, j);
    qsort(arr, cmp, i, b);
  }
}
...
qsort(ia, new IntegerComparator(), 0, ia.length-1);
GenericFunQuicksort.<Integer>qsort(ia, new IntegerComparator(), 0, ia.length-1);
```

Example 116 A Generic Quicksort Method for Comparable Values
This method sorts an array of type `T[]` whose elements of type `T` must be comparable to themselves. This is expressed by the method's parameter constraint as in example 110.

```
private static <T extends Comparable<T>> void qsort(T[] arr, int a, int b) {
  ...
  while (arr[i].compareTo(x) < 0) i++;
  while (x.compareTo(arr[j]) < 0) j--;
  ...
}
```

Example 117 A Generic Method in a Generic Class
The generic class MyLinkedList<T> in example 108 can be equipped with a generic method <U> map that takes an additional type parameter U and returns a new list of type MyLinkedList<U>. The generic interface MyList<T> is from example 112 and the generic interface Mapper<T,U> is from example 113.

```
class MyLinkedList<T> implements MyList<T> {
  ...
  public <U> MyList<U> map(Mapper<T,U> f) {        // Map f over all elements
    MyLinkedList<U> res = new MyLinkedList<U>();
    for (T x : this)
      res.add(f.call(x));
    return res;
  }
}
```

21.9   Wildcard Type Arguments

A *wildcard type* is a type expression that denotes some unknown type. A wildcard type can be used only as a type argument in a generic type instance, as in Shop<?> where Shop<T> is a generic type from example 118; a wildcard cannot be used as a type on its own. A wildcard type is useful when one must give a type argument in a generic type or method, but does want to specify the exact type. There are three forms of wildcard types:

```
<?>
<? extends tb>
<? super tb>
```

Here the tb is a type expression, possibly involving further occurrences of wildcard type expressions (which then stands for unrelated types). The first form of wildcard represents some unknown type; the second form represents some unknown type that is tb or a subtype of tb; and the third form represents some unknown type that is tb or a supertype of tb.

A wildcard type expression should not be confused with a type parameter constraint in the declaration of a generic type or method (section 21.5); in particular a parameter constraint cannot have the form T super tb.

Consider the Shop<T> example opposite, where a Shop<T> is a shop that deals in objects of type T.

First, a Shop<Car> is a shop to which we can sell objects of type Car (or a subclass); and when we buy from the shop we know that we get a Car or something that is a subtype of Car.

A Shop<?> is a shop that deals in some unknown type of object. The shop might be a Shop<Vehicle> or a Shop<Sedan> or a Shop<Painting>. Therefore we know only that what we buy from the shop is an Object; and we cannot sell anything to the shop at all, not knowing the type of objects it will accept.

A Shop<? extends Car> is a shop that deals in some unknown subtype of Car. Therefore what we buy from the shop must be a Car; but we cannot sell anything to the shop at all, not knowing the type Cars it will accept.

A Shop<? super Car> is a shop that deals in some unknown supertype of Car. Obviously, what we buy from the shop must be an Object, and we know that we can sell Cars (or even Sedans) to the shop.

A variable b of type Shop<?> can be given (assigned or passed) a value of type Shop<t> for any type t. A variable b of type Shop<? extends tb> can be assigned a value of type Shop<t> only if type t is a subtype of tb. For instance, a variable of type Shop<? extends Car> can be assigned a Shop<Sedan> or a Shop<Car> but not a Shop<Vehicle>. Conversely, a variable b of type Shop<? super tb> can be assigned a value of type Shop<t> only if type t is a supertype of tb. For instance, a variable of type Shop<? super Car> can be assigned a Shop<Car> or Shop<Vehicle> but not Shop<Sedan>. Thus the subtype relations between Shops are these:

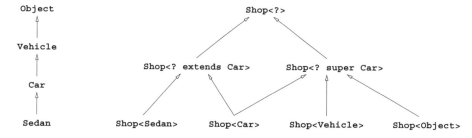

In general, the wildcard type <? extends tb> is useful as type argument when a value of a generic type must be usable as a producer of objects of type tb. Conversely, the wildcard type <? super tb> is useful as type argument when a value of a generic type must be usable as a consumer of objects of type tb.

Wildcards are used extensively in the parameter types and type constraints in the generic collection library (section 22). Examples 136 and 137 explain two of the more intricate cases.

Example 118 Wildcard Types

Assume we have three classes Vehicle, Car and Sedan, where Vehicle has subclass Car, and Car has subclass Sedan (a closed car). Now consider a generic class Shop<T> that represents a shop or broker from which we can buy and to which we can sell things of type T. A Shop<T> has a method T buyFrom() that allows us to buy a T from the shop, and a method void sellTo(T) that allows us to sell a T to the shop.

```
class Vehicle { }
class Car extends Vehicle { }
class Sedan extends Car { }
class Shop<T> {
  private T thing;
  public T buyFrom() { return thing; }
  public void sellTo(T thing) { this.thing = thing; }
}
```

The table below shows well-typed (+) and ill-typed (−) uses of variables b of the five types Shop, Shop<Car>, Shop<?>, Shop<? extends Car> and Shop<? super Car>. Note that Shop is the raw type underlying Shop<T>.

Operation \ Type of b	Shop	Shop<Car>	Shop<?>	Shop<? extends Car>	Shop<? super Car>
b = new Shop<Object>()	+	−	+	−	+
b = new Shop<Vehicle>()	+	−	+	−	+
b = new Shop<Car>()	+	+	+	+	+
b = new Shop<Sedan>()	+	−	+	+	−
b.sellTo(object)	+	−	−	−	−
b.sellTo(vehicle)	+	−	−	−	−
b.sellTo(car)	+	+	−	−	+
b.sellTo(sedan)	+	+	−	−	+
Object o = b.buyFrom()	+	+	+	+	+
Vehicle v = b.buyFrom()	−	+	−	+	−
Car c = b.buyFrom()	−	+	−	+	−
Sedan s = b.buyFrom()	−	−	−	−	−
b.sellTo(b.buyFrom())	+	+	−	−	−

For a variable b of raw type Shop, the sellTo method will accept any object at all, as would Shop<Object>. (But a new Shop<Car>() could not be assigned to a variable of type Shop<Object>). Although Car is a subclass of Object, Shop<Car> is not a subclass of Shop<Object>; see section 21.4.

For a Shop<Car>, the sellTo-method will accept a Car or any subclass such as Sedan, and the object returned by the buyFrom-method can be considered a Car or any superclass, such as Vehicle.

For a Shop<?>, the sellTo-method will accept neither Car nor Sedan nor Vehicle (because the actual element type T might be completely unrelated to these types; say, type Painting), and the object returned by the buyFrom-method could be assigned to a variable of type Object, but not Vehicle nor Car nor Sedan (again because the actual element type T might be completely unrelated to these types).

For a Shop<? extends Car>, the sellTo-method will accept neither Car nor Sedan nor Vehicle (because the actual element type T might be a subtype of Car unrelated to Sedan, say, Convertible). The object returned by the buyFrom-method can be considered a Car or any superclass, such as Vehicle.

For a Shop<? super Car>, the sellTo-method will accept a Car or any subclass such as Sedan, and the object returned by the buyFrom-method can be considered an Object, but not Vehicle nor Car nor Sedan (because the actual element type T might be a superclass of Vehicle, such as Mobile).

The expression b.sellTo(b.buyFrom()) is well-typed when b has type Shop or Shop<Car>, but ill-typed in the other cases, although a object returned by buyFrom would always be a suitable argument for sellTo.

21.10   The Raw Type

For every generic type there is an underlying *raw type*. For a generic class C<T1,...,Tn> the raw type is a non-generic class C which is a supertype of all type instances C<t1,...,tn> of the generic class C<T1,...,Tn>. For a generic interface I<T1,...,Tn> the raw type is an interface I which is a superinterface of all type instances I<t1,...,tn> of the generic interface I<T1,...,Tn>.

The raw type C is derived from the generic class declaration by *erasure*, as follows:

- If Ti is a type parameter of C<T1,...,Tn> without a constraint, then any use of Ti in the body of class C is replaced by Object.

- If Ti is a type parameter of C<T1,...,Tn> with constraints c_1 & c_2 & ... & c_n, then any use of Ti in the body of class C is replaced by c_1.

For this reason one sometimes sees constraints of the form Ti extends Object & c_2 & ... & c_n that begin with an apparently superfluous occurrence of Object.

21.11   The Implementation of Generic Types and Methods

Generic types and methods in Java resemble C++ type templates and function templates, and resemble generic types and methods in the C# 2.0 programming language. However, generic types and methods in Java 5.0 have been designed to allow programs that use generics to run on the same non-generic Java Virtual Machine as older Java programs. This design has several implications:

- Only reference types, not primitive types, can be used as generic type arguments. Thus a type parameter T must be instantiated with type Integer, not type int, and int values must be wrapped as Integer objects. This so-called boxed representation carries a certain overhead in execution time and space because Integer objects must be allocated on the heap to wrap int values, extra memory accesses are needed, and the int values must be unboxed before performing arithmetics or comparisons.

- There is a single type in the run-time system common to all the type instances C<t1,...,tn> of a generic type C<T1,...,Tn>, namely, the raw type C. In particular, all object instances of all type instances have the same field layout and contain the same bytecode instructions.

  Thus at run-time, the type instances Pair<String, Integer> and Pair<Date, String> in example 106 are actually represented by the same raw type Pair with fields of type Object. This loses some optimization opportunities that exist for C++ templates and for C# 2.0 generic types and methods.

- Overloading resolution of a method m or constructor does not take type arguments in m's parameter types into account and does not distinguish generic and raw types in m's parameter types. For example, these three methods are not considered distinct, and at most one of them can be declared in a given scope:

  ```
  void m(List xs) { ... }
  void m(List<Integer> xs) { ... }
  void m(List<String> xs) { ... }
  ```

- At run-time there is no information about the actual type arguments of a generic type or method. Therefore type parameters cannot be used in instanceof tests and only to a limited extent in reflection.

Nevertheless, Java's generic types and generic methods provide better compile-time type safety than C++, whose templates are typechecked only when type instances are created for given type parameters.

Example 119 Implementation by Type Erasure
The type erasure of example 111 is shown below. In other words, the JVM bytecode generated from that example is identical to that generated from the Java code below.

```
class Hold {
  private Object contents;
  public void set(Object x) { contents = x; }        // Note: no cast
  public Object get() { return contents; }
}
...
Hold h = new Hold();
h.set("foo");                      // Succeeds at run-time
h.get();                           // Succeeds at run-time
Integer i = (Integer)h.get();      // Legal, but fails at run-time
```

Example 120 Java Generics Limitation: Cannot Create Array with Generic Element Type
In declarations of fields, variables, parameters and return types, one can freely use array types whose element types are type parameters such as T, or type instances such as C<T> or C<Integer>. However, one cannot create (using new) an array whose element type is a type parameter or any kind of constructed type.

This is because Java (and C#) considers array type s[] to be a subtype of t[] whenever s and t are reference types and s is a subtype of t. This is safe only if at every array assignment arr[i] = e, it is checked that the run-time of e is a subtype of the actual element type of arr (section 8.1). This requires a representation of the element type to exist at run-time for every array. Since Java generics are implemented by type erasure, there exists no precise representation of the types T or C<T> or C<Integer> at run-time, so this information cannot be associated with an array type such as T[], and therefore the array element assignment check cannot be performed accurately. Therefore the creation of such arrays is rejected by the compiler.

By contrast, the type ArrayList<s> is *not* a subtype of ArrayList<t> when s is a subtype of t. Hence no check is needed at run-time when storing objects in the arraylist, and there is no need for a run-time representation of the arraylist's element type.

```
class F<T> {
  public void M() {
    T[] tarr;                              // Legal declaration
    G<T>[] ctarr;                          // Legal declaration
    G<Integer>[] ciarr;                    // Legal declaration
    // tarr = new T[5];                    // Illegal generic array creation
    // ctarr = new G<T>[5];                // Illegal generic array creation
    // ciarr = new G<Integer>[5];          // Illegal generic array creation

    ArrayList<T> tlist;                    // Legal declaration
    ArrayList<G<T>> ctlist;                // Legal declaration
    ArrayList<G<Integer>> cilist;          // Legal declaration
    tlist = new ArrayList<T>();            // Legal arraylist creation
    ctlist = new ArrayList<G<T>>();        // Legal arraylist creation
    cilist = new ArrayList<G<Integer>>();  // Legal arraylist creation
  }
}
```

22 Generic Collections and Maps (Java 5.0)

The Java class library package `java.util` provides collection classes and map (or dictionary) classes:

- A *collection*, described by generic interface Collection<T> (section 22.1), is used to group and handle many distinct *elements* of type T as a whole.

- A *list*, described by generic interface List<T> (section 22.2), is a collection whose elements can be traversed in insertion order. Implemented by the generic classes LinkedList<T> (for linked lists, double-ended queues, and stacks) and ArrayList<T> (for dynamically extensible arrays and stacks).

- A *set*, described by generic interface Set<T> (section 22.3), is a collection that cannot contain duplicate elements. Implemented by the generic classes HashSet<T> and LinkedHashSet<T>.

  A *sorted set*, described by generic interface SortedSet<T> (section 22.4), is a set whose elements are ordered: either the elements implement method `compareTo` specified by interface Comparable<T>, or the set's ordering is given explicitly by an object of type Comparator<T> (section 22.8). Implemented by generic class TreeSet<T>.

- A *map*, described by generic interface Map<K,V> (section 22.5), represents a mapping from a key of type K to at most one value of type V for each key. Implemented by the generic classes HashMap<K,V>, IdentityHashMap<K,V>, and LinkedHashMap<K,V>.

  A *sorted map*, described by generic interface SortedMap<K,V> (section 22.6), is a map whose keys are ordered, as for SortedSet<K>. Implemented by class TreeMap<K,V>.

The standard interfaces, intermediate abstract classes and concrete implementation classes are shown below. User-defined implementation classes can be conveniently defined as subclasses of the abstract classes, see the Java class library documentation on package `java.util` [3]. Solid arrows denote the subinterface and subclass relations, and dashed arrows indicate the "implements" relation between a class and an interface.

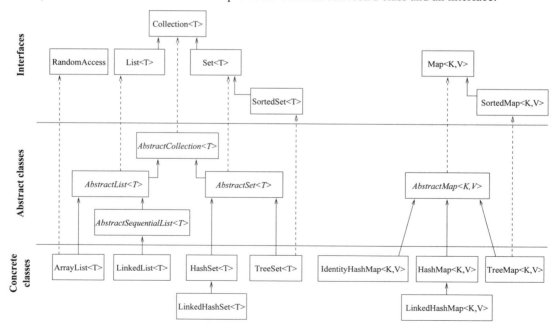

Example 121 Using the Concrete Collection and Map Classes
Here we create instances of five concrete collection classes with element type String, and add some elements to them. For each collection, we call method `traverse` in example 129 to print its elements.

We also create instances of three concrete map classes with keys and values of type String, and add some entries to them. For each map, we call `traverse` separately on its set of keys and its collection of values.

Note that TreeSet, which implements SortedSet, guarantees that the elements will be traversed in the order specified by the `compareTo` method (section 22.8) of the elements, and LinkedHashSet guarantees that the elements will be traversed in insertion order, whereas HashSet provides no such guarantee. Similarly, a TreeMap guarantees traversal in key order, and LinkedHashMap guarantees traversal in key insertion order, whereas HashMap does not guarantee any particular order.

```java
import java.util.*;

class CollectionAll {
  public static void main(String[] args) {
    List<String> list1 = new LinkedList<String>();
    list1.add("list"); list1.add("dup"); list1.add("x"); list1.add("dup");
    traverse(list1);                      // Must print: list dup x dup
    List<String> list2 = new ArrayList<String>();
    list2.add("list"); list2.add("dup"); list2.add("x"); list2.add("dup");
    traverse(list2);                      // Must print: list dup x dup
    Set<String> set1 = new HashSet<String>();
    set1.add("set"); set1.add("dup"); set1.add("x"); set1.add("dup");
    traverse(set1);                       // May print:  x dup set
    SortedSet<String> set2 = new TreeSet<String>();
    set2.add("set"); set2.add("dup"); set2.add("x"); set2.add("dup");
    traverse(set2);                       // Must print: dup set x
    LinkedHashSet<String> set3 = new LinkedHashSet<String>();
    set3.add("set"); set3.add("dup"); set3.add("x"); set3.add("dup");
    traverse(set3);                       // Must print: set dup x
    Map<String,String> m1 = new HashMap<String,String>();
    m1.put("map", "J"); m1.put("dup", "K"); m1.put("x", "M"); m1.put("dup", "L");
    traverse(m1.keySet());                // May print:  x dup map
    traverse(m1.values());                // May print:  M L J
    SortedMap<String,String> m2 = new TreeMap<String,String>();
    m2.put("map", "J"); m2.put("dup", "K"); m2.put("x", "M"); m2.put("dup", "L");
    traverse(m2.keySet());                // Must print: dup map x
    traverse(m2.values());                // Must print: L J M
    LinkedHashMap<String,String> m3 = new LinkedHashMap<String,String>();
    m3.put("map", "J"); m3.put("dup", "K"); m3.put("x", "M"); m3.put("dup", "L");
    traverse(m3.keySet());                // Must print: map dup x
    traverse(m3.values());                // Must print: J L M
  }

  static void traverse(Collection<String> coll) { ... }
}
```

22.1   Interface Collection<T>

The Collection<T> interface extends the Iterable<T> interface (section 22.7) and describes these methods:

- `boolean add(T o)` adds element o to the collection; returns `true` if the element was added, `false` if the collection disallows duplicates and contains an element equal to o already.

- `boolean addAll(Collection<? extends T> coll)` adds all elements of `coll` to the collection; returns `true` if any element was added.

- `void clear()` removes all elements from the collection.

- `boolean contains(T o)` returns `true` if any element of the collection equals o.

- `boolean containsAll(Collection<?> coll)` returns `true` if the collection contains all elements of `coll`.

- `boolean isEmpty()` returns `true` if the collection has no elements.

- `Iterator<T> iterator()` returns an iterator (section 22.7) over the elements of the collection.

- `boolean remove(Object o)` removes a single instance of element o from the collection; returns `true` if the collection contained such an element.

- `boolean removeAll(Collection<?> coll)` removes all those elements that are also in `coll`; returns `true` if any element was removed. After this operation, no element of the collection equals an element of `coll`.

- `boolean retainAll(Collection<?> coll)` retains only those elements that are also in `coll`; returns `true` if any element was removed. After this operation, every element of the collection equals some element of `coll`.

- `int size()` returns the number of elements in the collection.

- `Object[] toArray()` returns a new array containing all the elements of the collection.

- `<T> T[] toArray(T[] a)` works like the preceding, but the returned array's element type is the same as the element type of the given array a. Moreover, the elements are returned in the given array a if `a.length >= size()`, otherwise in a newly created array.

The element type T must be a reference type, so values of primitive type such as `int` must be boxed (as Integer) when inserted and unboxed when retrieved; in Java 5.0 this is done automatically (section 5.4).

A *view* of a collection co1 is a another collection co2 that refers to the same underlying data structure. As a consequence, modifications to co1 immediately affect co2, and modifications to co2 immediately affect co1.

An *unmodifiable collection* does not admit modification: the operations add, clear, remove, set, and so on throw UnsupportedOperationException. The utility class Collections (section 22.9) provides static methods to create an unmodifiable view of a given collection.

A *synchronized collection* is thread-safe: several concurrent threads can safely access and modify it. For efficiency, the standard collection classes are not synchronized, and concurrent modification of a collection may make its internal state inconsistent. The utility class Collections (section 22.9) provides static methods to create a synchronized view of a given collection. All concurrent access to a collection should go through its synchronized view. An iterator (section 22.7) obtained from a synchronized collection coll does not automatically provide synchronized iteration; one must use `synchronized (coll) { ... }` to explicitly ensure exclusive access to the collection during the execution of the block { ... } that performs the iteration.

22.2 Interface List<T> and Implementations LinkedList<T> and ArrayList<T>

The List<T> interface extends the Collection<T> interface with operations for position-based access using indexes 0, 1, 2, . . . and gives more precise specifications of some methods:

- `boolean add(T o)` adds element o at the end of the list. Returns true.

- `void add(int i, T o)` adds element o at position i, increasing the index of any element to the right by 1. Throws IndexOutOfBoundsException if `i<0` or `i>size()`.

- `boolean addAll(int i, Collection<? extends T> coll)` adds all elements of `coll` to the list, starting at position i; returns true if any element was added. Throws IndexOutOfBoundsException if `i<0` or `i>size()`.

- `boolean equals(Object o)` returns true if o is a List with equal elements in the same order.

- `T get(int i)` returns the element at index i; throws IndexOutOfBoundsException if `i<0` or `i>=size()`.

- `int hashCode()` returns the hash code of the list, which is a function of the hash codes of the elements and their order in the list.

- `int indexOf(Object o)` returns the least index i for which the element at position i equals o; returns −1 if the list does not contain such an element.

- `int lastIndexOf(Object o)` returns the greatest index i for which the element at position i equals o; returns −1 if the list does not contain such an element.

- `ListIterator<T> listIterator()` returns a bidirectional list iterator; see section 22.7.

- `T remove(int i)` removes the element at position i and returns it; or throws IndexOutOfBoundsException if `i<0` or `i>=size()`.

- `T set(int i, T o)` sets the element at position i to o and returns the element previously at position i; throws IndexOutOfBoundsException if `i<0` or `i>=size()`.

- `List<T> subList(int from, int to)` returns a list of the elements at positions `from..(to-1)`, as a view of the underlying list. Throws IndexOutOfBoundsException if `from<0` or `from>to` or `to>size()`.

The LinkedList<T> class implements all the operations described by the List interface and has the following constructors. The implementation is a doubly linked list, so elements can be accessed, added, and removed efficiently at either end of the list. It therefore provides additional methods for position-based get, add, and remove called `addFirst`, `addLast`, `getFirst`, `getLast`, `removeFirst`, and `removeLast`. The latter four throw NoSuchElementException if the list is empty.

- `LinkedList()` creates a new empty LinkedList<T>.

- `LinkedList(Collection<T> coll)` creates a new list containing the elements from `coll`'s iterator.

The ArrayList<T> class implements all the operations described by the List interface and has the following constructors. The implementation uses an underlying array (expanded as needed to hold the elements), which permits efficient position-based access anywhere in the list. Class ArrayList implements the RandomAccess interface just to indicate that element access by index is guaranteed to be fast, in contrast to LinkedList. The ArrayList class provides all the functionality provided originally (pre-Java 1.2) by the Vector class, which is a subclass of AbstractList and implements List and RandomAccess.

- `ArrayList()` creates a new empty ArrayList<T>.

- `ArrayList(Collection<T> coll)` creates a new list containing the elements from `coll`'s iterator.

22.3   Interface Set<T> and Implementations HashSet<T> and LinkedHashSet<T>

The Set<T> interface describes the same methods as the Collection<T> interface. The methods add and addAll must make sure that a set contains no duplicates: no two equal elements and at most one null element. Also, the methods equals and hashCode have more precise specifications for Set<T> objects:

- boolean equals(Object o) returns true if o is a Set with the same number of elements, and every element of o is also in this set.
- int hashCode() returns the hash code of the set: the sum of the hash codes of its non-null elements.

For Set arguments, addAll computes set union, containsAll computes set inclusion, removeAll computes set difference, and retainAll computes set intersection (example 138).

The HashSet<T> class implements the Set<T> interface and has the following constructors. Operations on a HashSet rely on the equals and hashCode methods of the element objects.

- HashSet() creates an empty set.
- HashSet(Collection<T> coll) creates a set containing the elements of coll, without duplicates.

The LinkedHashSet<T> class is a subclass of HashSet<T> and works the same way but additionally guarantees that its iterator traverses the elements in insertion order (rather than the unpredictable order provided by HashSet).

22.4   Interface SortedSet<T> and Implementation TreeSet<T>

The SortedSet<T> interface extends the Set<T> interface. Operations on a SortedSet rely on the natural ordering of the elements defined by their compareTo method, or on an explicit Comparator<T> object provided when the set was created (section 22.8), as for TreeSet<T> below.

- Comparator<? super T> comparator() returns the Comparator associated with this sorted set, or null if it uses the natural ordering (section 22.8) of the elements.
- T first() returns the least element; throws NoSuchElementException if the set is empty.
- SortedSet<T> headSet(T to) returns the set of all elements strictly less than to. The resulting set is a view of the underlying set.
- T last() returns the greatest element; throws NoSuchElementException if the set is empty.
- SortedSet<T> subSet(T from, T to) returns the set of all elements greater than or equal to from and strictly less than to. The resulting set is a view of the underlying set.
- SortedSet<T> tailSet(T from) returns the set of all elements greater than or equal to from. The resulting set is a view of the underlying set.

The TreeSet<T> class implements the SortedSet<T> interface and has the following constructors. The implementation uses balanced binary trees, so all operations are guaranteed to be efficient.

- TreeSet() creates an empty set, ordering elements using their compareTo method.
- TreeSet(Collection<? extends T> coll) creates a set containing the elements of coll, without duplicates, ordering elements using their compareTo method.
- TreeSet(Comparator<? super T> cmp) creates an empty set, ordering elements using cmp.
- TreeSet(SortedSet<T> s) creates a set containing the elements of s, ordering elements as in s.

Example 122 Set Membership Test Using HashSet or Binary Search
Imagine that we want to exclude Java reserved names (chapter 2) from the concordance built in example 127, so we need a fast way to recognize such names. Method `isKeyword1` uses a HashSet built from a 53-element array of Java keywords, whereas method `isKeyword2` uses binary search in the sorted array. The HashSet is two to five times faster in this case.

```
class SetMembership {
  final static String[] keywordarray =
    { "abstract", "assert", "boolean", "break", "byte", ..., "while" };
  final static Set<String> keywords
    = new HashSet<String>(Arrays.asList(keywordarray));

  static boolean isKeyword1(String id)
  { return keywords.contains(id); }

  static boolean isKeyword2(String id)
  { return Arrays.binarySearch(keywordarray, id) >= 0; }
}
```

Example 123 Using a LinkedHashSet to Remove Duplicates While Maintaining Item Order
Method `unique` takes an array of strings and returns a new array with the same strings in the same order but without duplicates. For instance, the array might hold names of files to be recompiled in a particular order, but possibly with the same file appearing multiple times. Clearly the order should be maintained but all occurrences except the first one should be removed. This is simply and efficiently done using a LinkedHashSet<String>, whereas a HashSet<String> would return the file names in some arbitrary order.

The call `toArray(new String[])` creates a new array with element type String, and copies the elements of `uniqueFiles` to that array; see section 22.1.

```
public static String[] unique(String[] filenames) {
  LinkedHashSet<String> uniqueFiles = new LinkedHashSet<String>();
  for (String filename : filenames)
    uniqueFiles.add(filename);
  return uniqueFiles.toArray(new String[0]);
}
```

Example 124 Using a TreeSet to Show a Range of File Names in Alphabetic Order
When file names are stored in a TreeSet, then one can efficiently extract a subrange of file names, and iteration over the set or a subrange will produce the file names in alphabetical (sorted) order. For instance, to extract all file names that begin with P or Q or R or S, one can compute `filenames.subSet("P", "T")`, the set of those strings greater than or equal to `"P"`, and strictly less than `"T"`.

```
SortedSet<String> filenames = new TreeSet<String>();
File cwd = new File(".");                 // Current working directory
for (File f : cwd.listFiles())
  filenames.add(f.getName());
for (String filename : filenames.subSet("P", "T"))
  System.out.println(filename);
```

22.5   Interface Map<K,V> and Implementation HashMap<K,V>

The Map<K,V> interface describes the following methods. A map can be considered a collection of entries, where an *entry* is a pair (k,v) of a key k of type K and a value v of type V. Both K and V must be reference types, so values of primitive type such as int must be boxed when inserted and unboxed when retrieved; in Java 5.0 this is done automatically (section 5.4). A map can contain no two entries with the same key.

- void clear() removes all entries from this map.
- boolean containsKey(Object k) returns true if the map has an entry with key k.
- boolean containsValue(Object v) returns true if the map has an entry with value v.
- Set<Map.Entry<K,V>> entrySet() returns a set view of the map's entries; each entry has type Map.Entry<K,V> (see below).
- boolean equals(Object o) returns true if o is a Map with the same entry set.
- V get(Object k) returns the value v in the entry (k, v) with key k, if any; otherwise null.
- int hashCode() returns the hash code for the map, computed as the sum of the hash codes of the entries returned by entrySet().
- boolean isEmpty() returns true if this map contains no entries; that is, if size() is zero.
- Set<K> keySet() returns a set view of the keys in the map.
- V put(K k, V v) modifies the map so that it contains the entry (k, v); returns the value previously associated with key k, if any; else returns null.
- void putAll(Map<? extends K, ? extends V> map) copies all entries from map to this map.
- V remove(Object k) removes the entry for key k from the map, if any; returns the value previously associated with k, if any; else returns null.
- int size() returns the number of entries, which equals the number of keys, in the map.
- Collection<V> values() returns a collection view of the values in the map.

The Map.Entry<K,V> interface (example 130) describes operations on map entries:

- K getKey() returns the key in this entry.
- V getValue() returns the value in this entry.

The HashMap<K,V> class implements the Map<K,V> interface and has the following constructors. Operations on a HashMap rely on the equals and hashCode methods of the key objects.

- HashMap() creates an empty HashMap.
- HashMap(Map<? extends K, ? extends V> map) creates a HashMap<K,V> containing same the entries as map.

The LinkedHashMap<K,V> class is a subclass of HashMap<K,V> and works the same way but additionally guarantees that its iterator traverses the entries in key insertion order (rather than the unpredictable order provided by HashMap). It was introduced in Java 1.4.

The IdentityHashMap<K,V> class implements the Map<K,V> interface but compares keys using reference equality (==) instead of the equals method.

Example 125 Storing the Result of a Database Query

This method executes a database query, using classes from the `java.sql` package. It returns the result of the query as an ArrayList with one element for each row in the result. Each row is stored as a HashMap, mapping a result field name to an object (e.g., an Integer or String) holding the value of that field in that row. This is a simple and useful way to separate the database query from the processing of the query result (but it may be too inefficient if the query result is very large). The row list returned by `getRows` could be printed by method `printNameAndMsg`.

```
static ArrayList<Map<String,Object>> getRows(Connection conn, String query)
  throws SQLException
{
  Statement stmt = conn.createStatement();
  ResultSet rset = stmt.executeQuery(query);
  ResultSetMetaData rsmd = rset.getMetaData();
  int columncount = rsmd.getColumnCount();
  ArrayList<Map<String,Object>> queryResult = new ArrayList<Map<String,Object>>();
  while (rset.next()) {
    Map<String,Object> row = new HashMap<String,Object>();
    for (int i=1; i<=columncount; i++)
      row.put(rsmd.getColumnName(i), rset.getObject(i));
    queryResult.add(row);
  }
  return queryResult;
}
static void printNameAndMsg(Collection<Map<String,Object>> coll) {
  for (Map<String,Object> row : coll)
    System.out.println(row.get("name") + ": " + row.get("msg"));
}
```

Example 126 From Weekday Name to Weekday Number Using a HashMap

Method `wdayno5` behaves the same as those in examples 64 and 72, but uses a HashMap to map a string to an integer instead of `if` statements or a `while` loop. A HashMap is often faster, especially when the number of strings is large. The HashMap is initialized once using a static initializer block (section 9.13) and should be private to prevent accidental modification. There is an implicit unboxing from Integer to `int` in `wdayno5`.

```
class C {
  private static final HashMap<String,Integer> wdayNumber = new HashMap<String,Integer>();
  static { // Static initializer block, executed once
    int wdayno = 0;
    String[] wdays =
      { "Monday", "Tuesday", "Wednesday", "Thursday", "Friday", "Saturday", "Sunday" };
    for (String wday : wdays)
      wdayNumber.put(wday, wdayno++);
  }
  public static int wdayno5(String wday) {
    Integer res = wdayNumber.get(wday);
    return res == null ? -1 : res;
  }
  ...
}
```

22.6 Interface SortedMap<K,V> and Implementation TreeMap<K,V>

The SortedMap<K,V> interface extends the Map<K,V> interface. Operations on a SortedMap rely on the natural ordering of the keys defined by their `compareTo` method or on an explicit Comparator<K> object provided when the map was created (section 22.8), as for TreeMap<K,V> below.

- Comparator<? super K> comparator() returns the Comparator associated with this sorted map, or null if it uses the natural ordering (section 22.8) of the keys.

- K firstKey() returns the least key in this sorted map; throws NoSuchElementException if the map is empty.

- SortedMap<K,V> headMap(K to) returns the sorted map of all entries whose keys are strictly less than to. The resulting map is a view of the underlying map.

- K lastKey() returns the greatest key in this sorted map; throws NoSuchElementException if the map is empty.

- SortedMap<K,V> subMap(K from, K to) returns the sorted map of all entries whose keys are greater than or equal to from and strictly less than to. The resulting map is a view of the underlying map.

- SortedMap<K,V> tailMap(K from) returns the sorted map of all entries whose keys are greater than or equal to from. The resulting map is a view of the underlying map.

The TreeMap<K,V> class implements the SortedMap<K,V> interface and has the following constructors. The implementation uses balanced ordered binary trees, so all operations are guaranteed to be efficient.

- TreeMap() creates an empty map, ordering entries using the `compareTo` method of the keys.

- TreeMap(Map<? extends K, ? extends V>) creates a map containing the entries of map, ordering entries using the `compareTo` method of the keys.

- TreeMap(Comparator<? super K> cmp) creates an empty map, ordering entries using `cmp` on the keys.

- TreeMap(SortedMap<? extends K, ? extends V> s) creates a map containing the entries of s, ordering entries as in s.

Example 127 Building a Concordance

This method reads words (alphanumeric tokens) from a text file and creates a concordance, which shows for each word the line numbers of its occurrences. The resulting concordance index is a SortedMap from String to SortedSet of Integer. Example 130 shows how to print the resulting concordance.

```
static SortedMap<String,SortedSet<Integer>> buildIndex(String filename)
  throws IOException
{
  Reader r = new BufferedReader(new FileReader(filename));
  StreamTokenizer stok = new StreamTokenizer(r);
  stok.quoteChar('"'); stok.ordinaryChars('!', '/');
  stok.nextToken();
  SortedMap<String,SortedSet<Integer>> index = new TreeMap<String,SortedSet<Integer>>();
  while (stok.ttype != StreamTokenizer.TT_EOF) {
    if (stok.ttype == StreamTokenizer.TT_WORD) {
      SortedSet<Integer> ts;
      if (index.containsKey(stok.sval))        // If word has a set, get it
        ts = index.get(stok.sval);
      else {
        ts = new TreeSet<Integer>();           // Otherwise create one
        index.put(stok.sval, ts);
      }
      ts.add(stok.lineno());
    }
    stok.nextToken();
  }
  return index;
}
```

Example 128 Obtaining a Submap

A date book is a sorted map whose keys are Time objects (example 133). Using `tailMap` we can extract that part of the date book that concerns times on or after 12:00:

```
SortedMap<Time,String> datebook = new TreeMap<Time,String>();
datebook.put(new Time(12, 30), "Lunch");
datebook.put(new Time(15, 30), "Afternoon coffee break");
datebook.put(new Time( 9,  0), "Lecture");
datebook.put(new Time(13, 15), "Board meeting");
SortedMap<Time,String> pm = datebook.tailMap(new Time(12, 0));
for (Map.Entry<Time,String> entry : pm.entrySet())
  System.out.println(entry.getKey() + " " + entry.getValue());
```

22.7   Going Through a Collection: Interfaces Iterator<T> and Iterable<T>

The interfaces Iterator<T> and Iterable<T> provide a convenient way to go through the elements of a collection or the entries of a map. Namely, an Iterator<T> has methods `hasNext` and `next` to go through a sequence of elements, and an Iterable<T> has a method `iterator` that returns a new Iterator<T>.

The elements of an iterable is usually traversed using the enhanced `for` statement (section 12.5.2) as shown in examples 129 and 130, but one can also explicitly get an iterator from the iterable and then use that in a `while` or `for` loop, as shown in examples 71 and 74.

The Iterator<T> interface from package `java.util` describes the following methods:

- `boolean hasNext()` returns `true` if a call to `next()` will return a new element.

- `T next()` returns the next element and advances past that element, if any; throws NoSuchElementException if there is no next element.

- `void remove()` removes the last element returned by the iterator; throws IllegalStateException if no element has been returned by the iterator yet, or if the element has been removed already. If element removal is not supported, it throws UnsupportedOperationException.

The Iterable<T> interface (introduced in Java 5.0) from package `java.lang` describes the following method:

- `Iterator<T> iterator()` returns a new iterator for this iterable.

All collections are directly iterable because the interface Collection<T> has superinterface Iterable<T> . The entries of a map can be iterated over because interface Map<K,V> describes a method `entrySet` that returns a Set<Map.Entry<K,V>>, which implements Iterable<Map.Entry<K,V>>.

An iterator obtained from a List will traverse the elements in the order of the list. An iterator obtained from SortedSet, or from the keys or values of a SortedMap, will traverse the elements in the order of the set elements or the map keys. An iterator obtained from a HashSet will traverse the elements in some unpredictable order. An Iterator provides all the functionality originally provided by the Enumeration interface (before Java 1.2) but has different method names.

When iterating over a collection or map, the underlying collection should not be modified except through the iterator's `remove` method. If it is modified in any other way, the result is unpredictable. In fact, the concrete classes ArrayList, LinkedList, HashMap, HashSet, TreeMap, and TreeSet produce fail-fast iterators: if the underlying collection is structurally modified (except by the iterator's `remove` method) after an iterator has been obtained, then a ConcurrentModificationException is thrown by the next call to `hasNext` or `next`.

The ListIterator<T> interface from package `java.util` extends interface Iterator<T> and permits insertion, update, and bidirectional traversal of an underlying list:

- `void add(T o)` inserts the element o just before the list cursor, that is, between the elements that would be returned by calls to `previous` and `next`. If at the head or end of the list, inserts the element before the head or after the end. A subsequent call to `previous` will return the new element.

- `boolean hasPrevious()` returns true if a call to `previous()` would return an element.

- `int nextIndex()` returns the list index of the item that would be returned by a call to `next`.

- `T previous()` returns the element after the list cursor (if any), and moves the cursor one element closer to the head of the list. Throws NoSuchElementException if the cursor cannot be moved back.

- `int previousIndex()` returns the list index of the item that would be returned by a call to `previous`.

Example 129 Iteration over an Iterable Collection

This method uses the enhanced `for` statement (section 12.5.2) to iterate over a collection `coll` and print its elements. The method is called in example 121. Examples 71 and 74 make explicit use of an iterator.

```
static void traverse(Collection<String> coll) {
  for (String elem : coll)
    System.out.print(elem + " ");
  System.out.println();
}
```

Example 130 Printing a Concordance Using Iterables

The map `index` is assumed to be a concordance as created in example 127. Method `printIndex` prints an alphabetical list of the words, and for each word, its line numbers. The foreach statements (section 12.5.2) create one iterator to go through the words, and for each word, a separate iterator to go through its line numbers.

```
static void printIndex(SortedMap<String,SortedSet<Integer>> index) {
  for (Map.Entry<String,SortedSet<Integer>> entry : index.entrySet()) {
    System.out.print(entry.getKey() + ": ");
    SortedSet<Integer> lineNoSet = entry.getValue();
    for (int lineno : lineNoSet)
      System.out.print(lineno + " ");
    System.out.println();
  }
}
```

Example 131 A Method Returning an Iterable

A call `fromTo(m,n)` returns an Iterable<Integer> from which one can obtain an Iterator<Integer> from which one can obtain the sequence of integers from m to n. Examples 70, 71 and 74 show various ways to use the iterable. It is created as an instance of a local class FromToIterable that implements Iterable<Integer> whose `iterator` method creates an instance of the local class FromToIterator that implements Iterator<Integer>. The same effect can be achieved more compactly by using anonymous local inner classes in the style of example 41, but that hardly makes the example clearer.

```
public static Iterable<Integer> fromTo(final int m, final int n) {
  class FromToIterator implements Iterator<Integer> {       // local class
    private int i = m;
    public boolean hasNext() { return i <= n; }
    public Integer next() {
      if (i <= n)
        return i++;
      else
        throw new NoSuchElementException();
    }
    public void remove() { throw new UnsupportedOperationException(); }
  }
  class FromToIterable implements Iterable<Integer> {       // local class
    public Iterator<Integer> iterator() {
      return new FromToIterator();
    }
  }
  return new FromToIterable();
}
```

22.8 Equality, Hash Codes, and Comparison

The elements of a collection must have a sensible `equals` method. If the elements have a sensible `hashCode` method, they can be used as HashSet elements or HashMap keys. If they have a `compareTo` method as described by the `java.lang.Comparable` interface, they can be used as TreeSet elements or TreeMap keys.

All classes have default implementations of the `equals` and `hashCode` methods, inherited from class Object. Most classes should override them to provide sensible notions of equality and hashcodes. If a class overrides either method, it should override also the other one, satisfying the requirements below.

The primitive type wrapper classes (section 5.4) and the String class all have sensible `equals`, `hashCode`, and `compareTo` methods, and so can be used as elements of collections and as keys in maps.

- `boolean equals(Object o)` determines the equality of two objects. It is used by ArrayList, LinkedList, HashSet, and HashMap. It should satisfy `o.equals(o)`; *not* `o.equals(null)`; if `o1.equals(o2)`, then also `o2.equals(o1)`; and if `o1.equals(o2)` and `o2.equals(o3)`, then also `o1.equals(o3)` for non-null `o1`, `o2`, and `o3`.

- `int hashCode()` returns the hash code of an object. It is used by HashSet and HashMap. It should satisfy that if `o1.equals(o2)`, then `o1.hashCode()==o2.hashCode()`.

The generic interface Comparable<T> from package `java.lang` describes a single method:

- `int compareTo(T o)` performs a three-way comparison of two objects: `o1.compareTo(o2)` is negative if `o1` is less than `o2`, zero if `o1` and `o2` are equal, and positive if `o1` is greater than `o2`.

  It is called the *natural ordering* of elements and is used for instance by TreeSet and TreeMap unless a Comparator was given when the set or map was created. It should satisfy that `o1.compareTo(o2)==0` whenever `o1.equals(o2)`.

The generic interface Comparator<T> from package `java.util` describes two methods:

- `int compare(T o1, T o2)` performs a three-way comparison of two objects: it is negative if `o1` is less than `o2`, zero if `o1` and `o2` are equal, and positive if `o1` is greater than `o2`. It can be used to define nonstandard element orderings when creating TreeSets and TreeMaps (see example 135). It should satisfy that `compare(o1, o2)==0` whenever `o1.equals(o2)`.

- `boolean equals(Object otherComparator)` overrides `equals` from Object. A comparator can override it to specify when it is equivalent to a given `otherComparator`. That is, `cmp1.equals(cmp2)` may return true if for all objects `o1` and `o2`, the sign of `cmp1(o1,o2)` is the same as that of `cmp2(o1,o2)`.

Example 132 A Comparator for the Integer Class

```
class IntegerComparator implements Comparator<Integer> {
  public int compare(Integer v1, Integer v2) {
    return v1 < v2 ? -1 : v1 > v2 ? +1 : 0;
} }
```

Example 133 A Time Class Implementing Comparable<Time>
A Time object represents the time of day 00:00–23:59. The method call t1.compareTo(t2) returns a negative number if t1 is before t2, a positive number if t1 is after t2, and zero if they are the same time.

```
class Time implements Comparable<Time> {
  public final int hh, mm;           // 24-hour clock
  public Time(int hh, int mm) { this.hh = hh; this.mm = mm; }
  public int compareTo(Time t) {
    return hh != t.hh ? hh - t.hh : mm - t.mm;
  }
  public boolean equals(Object o) { ... }       // See below
  public int hashCode() { return 60 * hh + mm; }
}
```

Example 134 An equals Method for the Time Class
First, equals in example 133 should quickly deal with the frequent case of comparing an object to itself. Next, if o is null, or if the run-time class of this is different from the run-time class of o, the result must be false. Finally, if o is non-null and has the same run-time class as this, then compare the fields for equality.

It is a common mistake to use argument type Time instead of Object. But then the method will not be called (by the hashset implementation, for instance) because it does not override equals(Object).

```
public boolean equals(Object o) {              // Note: Object, not Time
  if (this == o)                               // Fast and frequent case
    return true;
  if (o == null || this.getClass() != o.getClass()) // null or different classes
    return false;
  Time t = (Time)o;                            // Now, o instanceof Time
  return hh == t.hh && mm == t.mm;
}
```

Example 135 A Comparator for the String Class
The concordance in example 127 uses the built-in compareTo method of String, which orders all upper case letters before all lowercase letters: "Create" before "add" before "create". The Comparator class below puts strings that differ only in case next to each other: "add" before "Create" before "create".

To use it in example 127, replace new TreeMap<String,SortedSet<Integer>>() in that example by new TreeMap<String,SortedSet<Integer>>(new IgnoreCaseComparator()).

It is often preferable to specify the ordering separately by a comparator rather than using the default comparer of a comparable class, especially if several different comparators may be relevant.

```
class IgnoreCaseComparator implements Comparator<String> {
  public int compare(String s1, String s2) {
    int res = s1.compareToIgnoreCase(s2);
    return res != 0 ? res : s1.compareTo(s2);
  }
}
```

22.9   The Utility Class Collections

Class java.util.Collections provides static utility methods. The methods `binarySearch`, `max`, `min`, and `sort` also have versions that take an extra Comparator<? super T> argument and use it to compare elements.

There are static methods similar to `synchronizedList` and `unmodifiableList` for creating a synchronized or unmodifiable view (section 22.1) of a Collection, Set, SortedSet, Map, or SortedMap.

- `static <T extends Comparable<? super T>> int binarySearch(List<? extends T> lst, T k)` returns an index i>=0 for which `lst.get(i)` is equal to k, if any; otherwise returns i<0 such that `(-i-1)` would be the proper position for k. This is fast for ArrayList but slow for LinkedList. The list lst must be sorted, as by `sort(lst)`.

- `static <T> void copy(List<? super T> dst, List<? extends T> src)` adds all elements from src to dst, in order.

- `static <T> Enumeration<T> enumeration(Collection<T> coll)` returns an enumeration of coll.

- `static <T> void fill(List<? super T> lst, T o)` sets all elements of lst to o.

- `static <T extends Comparable<? super T>> T max(Collection<? extends T> coll)` returns the greatest element of coll. Throws NoSuchElementException if coll is empty.

- `static <T extends Comparable<? super T>> min(Collection<? extends T> coll)` returns the least element of coll. Throws NoSuchElementException if coll is empty.

- `static <T> List<T> nCopies(int n, T o)` returns an unmodifiable list with n copies of o.

- `static <T> boolean replaceAll(List<T> lst, T o1, T o2)` replaces all elements equal to o1 by o2 in lst; returns true if an element was replaced.

- `static void reverse(List<?> lst)` reverses the order of the elements in lst.

- `static <T> Comparator<T> reverseOrder()` returns a comparator that is the reverse of the natural ordering implemented by the compareTo method of elements or keys.

- `static void rotate(List<?> lst, int d)` rotates lst right by d positions, so -1 rotates left by one position. Rotates a sublist if applied to a sublist view (section 22.2).

- `static void shuffle(List<?> lst)` randomly permutes the elements of lst.

- `static void shuffle(List<?> lst, Random rnd)` randomly permutes the elements of lst using rnd to generate random numbers.

- `static <T> Set<T> singleton(T o)` returns an unmodifiable set containing only o.

- `static <T> List<T> singletonList(T o)` returns an unmodifiable list containing only o.

- `static <K,V> Map<K,V> singletonMap(K k, V v)` returns an unmodifiable map containing only the entry (k, v).

- `static <T extends Comparable<? super T>> void sort(List<T> lst)` sorts lst using merge-sort and the natural element ordering. This sorting algorithm is stable and is fast on all Lists.

- `static void swap(List<?> lst, int i, int j)` exchanges the list elements at positions i and j. It throws IndexOutOfBoundsException unless 0 <= i,j and i,j < lst.size().

- `static List<T> synchronizedList(List<T> lst)` returns a synchronized view of lst.

- `static List<T> unmodifiableList(List<T> lst)` returns an unmodifiable view of lst.

Example 136 Understanding the Type of the `Collections.binarySearch` Method
The generic method `binarySearch` has a type parameter T whose constraint involves a wildcard:

```
static <T extends Comparable<? super T>> int binarySearch(...)
```

The constraint says that type T must be a subtype of `Comparable<? super T>`. In other words, T or a supertype of T must have `compareTo` method, and that method's argument type must be T or a supertype of T; in any case that method can take a T object as argument.

For instance, assume that class Vehicle from example 118 implements Comparable<Vehicle>. Then the subclass Car also implements Comparable<Vehicle>, and so when T is Car, the unknown type that the wildcard (?) stands for could be Vehicle, satisfying the constraint on T.

Continuing with this scenario, consider the wildcard type in the `lst` parameter of `binarySearch`:

```
static ... int binarySearch(List<? extends T> lst, T k)
```

This means that `lst` may be any List whose element type is a subtype of T (which we assumed to be Car). For instance, that subtype could be Sedan from example 118. Taken together this means that method `binarySearch` can be applied to an argument `lst` of type List<Car> and an argument `k` of type Sedan, just because objects of their superclass Vehicle are comparable to themselves.

Note that if the signature of `binarySearch` had been more straightforward and less permissive, such as:

```
static <T extends Comparable<T>> int binarySearch(List<T> lst, T k)
```

then one could not apply the method to arguments of type List<Car> and Sedan. However, it could still be applied to List<Vehicle> and Sedan, because Vehicle implements Comparable<Vehicle> and Sedan is a subclass of Vehicle.

Example 137 Understanding the Type of the `Collections.copy` Method
The generic method `copy` uses two wildcards in its parameters:

```
static <T> void copy(List<? super T> dst, List<? extends T> src)
```

The parameter `dst` must be a List whose element type is a supertype of T, and the parameter `src` must be a List whose element type is a subtype of T. Thus even when T is Car, the `dst` could have type List<Vehicle> and the `src` could have type List<Sedan>, where the types Vehicle, Car and Sedan are from example 118. Note that different occurrences of the wildcard (?) may stand for different unknown types; for instance, Vehicle and Sedan.

The use of two rather than one wildcard in the type for `copy` provides a pleasant symmetry, or lack of bias towards either `dst` or `src`. But in fact this signature, with only one wildcard, would permit basically the same method calls:

```
static <U> void copy(List<? super U> dst, List<U> src)
```

In this case the type argument U must be instantiated to the subtype of T used for the `src` parameter in the previous signature.

22.10   Choosing the Right Collection Class or Map Class

The proper choice of a collection or map class depends on the operations you need to perform on it, and how frequent those operations are. There is no universal best choice.

- LinkedList (section 22.2) or ArrayList (section 22.2 and example 125) should be used for collecting elements for sequential iteration in index order, allowing duplicates.

- HashSet (section 22.3 and example 122) and HashMap (section 22.5 and example 125) are good default choices when random access by element or key is needed, and sequential access in element or key order is not needed. LinkedHashSet (example 123) and LinkedHashMap additionally guarantee sequential access (using their iterators) in element or key insertion order.

- TreeSet (section 22.4 and example 127) or TreeMap (section 22.6 and example 127) should be used for random access by element or key as well as for iteration in element or key order.

- LinkedList, not ArrayList, should be used for worklist algorithms (example 138), queues, double-ended queues, and stacks.

- ArrayList, not LinkedList, should be used for random access get(i) or set(i, o) by index.

- HashSet or HashMap should be used for sets or maps whose elements or keys are collections, because the collection classes implement useful hashCode methods (example 139).

- For maps whose keys are small non-negative integers, use ordinary arrays (chapter 8).

The running time or *time complexity* of an operation on a collection is usually given in O notation, as a function of the size n of the collection. Thus $O(1)$ means *constant time*, $O(\log n)$ means *logarithmic time* (time proportional to the logarithm of n), and $O(n)$ means *linear time* (time proportional to n). For accessing, adding, or removing an element, these roughly correspond to *very fast, fast*, and *slow*.

In the following table, n is the number of elements in the collection, i is an integer index, and d is the distance from an index i to the nearest end of a list, that is, $\min(i, n-i)$. Thus adding or removing an element of a LinkedList is fast near both ends of the list, where d is small, but for an ArrayList it is fast only near the back end, where $n-i$ is small. The subscript a indicates *amortized complexity*: over a long sequence of operations, the average time per operation is $O(1)$, although any single operation could take time $O(n)$.

Operation	LinkedList	ArrayList	HashSet LinkedHashSet	TreeSet	HashMap LinkedHashMap	TreeMap
add(o) (last)	$O(1)$	$O(1)_a$	$O(1)_a$	$O(\log n)$		
add(i,o)	$O(d)$	$O(n-i)_a$				
addFirst(o)	$O(1)$					
put(k,v)					$O(1)_a$	$O(\log n)$
remove(o)	$O(n)$	$O(n)$	$O(1)$	$O(\log n)$	$O(1)$	$O(\log n)$
remove(i)	$O(d)$	$O(n-i)$				
removeFirst()	$O(1)$					
contains(o)	$O(n)$	$O(n)$	$O(1)$	$O(\log n)$		
containsKey(o)					$O(1)$	$O(\log n)$
containsValue(o)					$O(n)$	$O(n)$
indexOf(o)	$O(n)$	$O(n)$				
get(i)	$O(d)$	$O(1)$				
set(i,o)	$O(d)$	$O(1)$				
get(o)					$O(1)$	$O(\log n)$

Example 138 A Worklist Algorithm

Some algorithms use a *worklist*, containing subproblems still to be solved. For instance, given a set `ss` of sets of Integers, compute its intersection closure: the least set `tt` such that `ss` is a subset of `tt` and such that for any two sets `s` and `t` in `tt`, their intersection `s ∩ t` is also in `tt`. For instance, if `ss` is {{2,3},{1,3},{1,2}}, then `tt` is {{2,3},{1,3},{1,2},{3},{2},{1},{}}.

The set `tt` may be computed by putting all elements of `ss` in a worklist, then repeatedly selecting an element `s` from the worklist, adding it to `tt`, and for every set `t` already in `tt`, adding the intersection of `s` and `t` to the worklist if not already in `tt`. When the worklist is empty, `tt` is intersection-closed.

The epsilon closure of a state of a nondeterministic finite automaton (NFA) may be computed using the same approach; see the full program text underlying example 139.

```
static <T> Set<Set<T>> intersectionClose(Set<Set<T>> ss) {
  LinkedList<Set<T>> worklist = new LinkedList<Set<T>>(ss);
  Set<Set<T>> tt = new HashSet<Set<T>>();
  while (!worklist.isEmpty()) {
    Set<T> s = worklist.removeLast();
    for (Set<T> t : tt) {
      Set<T> ts = new TreeSet<T>(t);
      ts.retainAll(s);                   // ts is the intersection of t and s
      if (!tt.contains(ts))
        worklist.add(ts);
    }
    tt.add(s);
  }
  return tt;
}
```

Example 139 Using Sets as Keys in a HashMap

The standard algorithm for turning a nondeterministic finite automaton (NFA) into a deterministic finite automaton (DFA) creates composite automaton states that are sets of integers. It is preferable to replace such composite states by simple integers. Method `mkRenamer` takes as argument a collection of composite states and returns a renamer, which is a map from composite states (Set of Integer) to simple states (Integer).

Method `rename` takes as arguments a renamer and a transition (which is a Map from Set of Integer to Map from String to Set of Integer) and performs the actual renaming, returning a renamed transition. The method is included here to show that type instances can be arbitrarily complex.

```
static Map<Set<Integer>,Integer> mkRenamer(Collection<Set<Integer>> states) {
  Map<Set<Integer>,Integer> renamer = new HashMap<Set<Integer>,Integer>();
  for (Set<Integer> k : states)
    renamer.put(k, renamer.size());
  return renamer;
}

static Map<Integer,Map<String,Integer>>
  rename(Map<Set<Integer>,Integer> renamer,
         Map<Set<Integer>,Map<String,Set<Integer>>> trans)
{
  Map<Integer,Map<String,Integer>> newtrans = new HashMap<Integer,Map<String,Integer>>();
  ...
  return newtrans;
}
```

23   Input and Output

Sequential input and output uses objects called *streams*. There are two kinds of streams: *character streams* and *byte streams*, also called text streams and binary streams. Character streams are used for input from text files and human-readable output to text files, printers, and so on, using 16-bit Unicode characters. Byte streams are used for compact and efficient input and output of primitive data (int, double, ...) as well as objects and arrays, in machine-readable form.

There are separate classes for handling character streams and byte streams. The classes for character input and output are called Readers and Writers. The classes for byte input and output are called InputStreams and OutputStreams. This chapter describes input and output using the java.io package. Java 1.4 and later provide additional facilities in package java.nio, not described here.

One can create subclasses of the stream classes, overriding inherited methods to obtain specialized stream classes. We shall not further discuss how to do that here.

The four stream class hierarchies are shown in the following table, with related input and output classes shown on the same line. The table shows, for instance, that BufferedReader and FilterReader are subclasses of Reader, and that LineNumberReader is a subclass of BufferedReader. Abstract classes are shown in *italics*.

	Input Streams	Output Streams
Character Streams	*Reader*	*Writer*
	BufferedReader	BufferedWriter
	LineNumberReader	
	FilterReader	*FilterWriter*
	PushBackReader	
	InputStreamReader	OutputStreamWriter
	FileReader	FileWriter
	PipedReader	PipedWriter
		PrintWriter
	CharArrayReader	CharArrayWriter
	StringReader	StringWriter
Byte Streams	*InputStream*	*OutputStream*
	ByteArrayInputStream	ByteArrayOutputStream
	FileInputStream	FileOutputStream
	FilterInputStream	FilterOutputStream
	BufferedInputStream	BufferedOutputStream
	DataInputStream	DataOutputStream
	PushBackInputStream	
		PrintStream
	ObjectInputStream	ObjectOutputStream
	PipedInputStream	PipedOutputStream
	SequenceInputStream	
	RandomAccessFile	

The classes DataInputStream, ObjectInputStream, and RandomAccessFile implement the interface DataInput, and the classes DataOutputStream, ObjectOutputStream and RandomAccessFile implement the interface DataOutput (section 23.11).

The class ObjectInputStream implements interface ObjectInput, and class ObjectOutputStream implements interface ObjectOutput (section 23.12).

23.1   Creating Streams from Other Streams

A stream may either be created outright (e.g., a FileInputStream may be created and associated with a named file on disk, for reading from that file) or it may be created from an existing stream to provide additional features (e.g., a BufferedInputStream may be created from a FileInputStream, for more efficient input). In any case, an input stream or reader has an underlying source of data to read from, and an output stream or writer has an underlying sink of data to write to. The following figure shows how streams may be defined in terms of existing streams, or in terms of other data.

The stream classes are divided along two lines: character streams (top) versus byte streams (bottom), and input streams (left) versus output streams (right). The arrows show what streams can be created from other streams. For instance, the arrow from InputStream to InputStreamReader shows that one can create an InputStreamReader from an InputStream. The arrow from Reader to BufferedReader shows that one can create a BufferedReader from a Reader. Since an InputStreamReader is a Reader, one can create a BufferedReader from an existing InputStream (such as `System.in`) in two steps, as shown in example 140. On the other hand, there is no way to create a PipedOutputStream from a File or a file name; a PipedOutputStream must be created outright, or from an existing PipedInputStream, and similarly for other pipes (section 23.16).

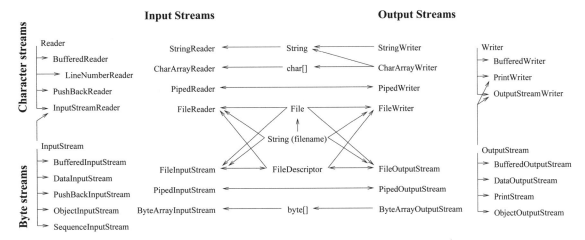

Example 140 A Complete Input-Output Example

```
import java.io.*;
class BasicIOExample {
  public static void main(String[] args) throws IOException {
    BufferedReader r = new BufferedReader(new InputStreamReader(System.in));
    int count = 0;
    String s = r.readLine();
    while (s != null && !s.equals("")) {
      count++;
      s = r.readLine();
    }
    System.out.println("You entered " + count + " nonempty lines");
} }
```

23.2   Kinds of Input and Output Methods

The following table summarizes the naming conventions for methods of the input and output classes as well as their main characteristics, such as their end-of-stream behavior.

Method Name	Effect
`read`	Inputs characters from a Reader (section 23.4) or inputs bytes from an InputStream (section 23.9). It *blocks*, that is, does not return, until some input is available; returns -1 on end-of-stream.
`write`	Outputs characters to a Writer (section 23.5) or outputs bytes to an OutputStream (section 23.10).
`format`	Uses a formatting string to convert values to textual representation and then outputs that representation to a PrintWriter or PrintStream (section 7.1).
`print`	Converts a value (`int`, `double`, ..., Object) to textual representation and outputs it to a PrintWriter or PrintStream (section 23.6).
`println`	Same as `print` but outputs a newline after printing.
`printf`	Same as `format` (section 7.1).
`read`*t*	Inputs a value of primitive type *t* from a DataInput stream (section 23.11). Blocks until some input is available; throws EOFException on end-of-stream.
`write`*t*	Outputs a primitive value of primitive type *t* to a DataOutput stream (section 23.11).
`readObject`	Deserializes objects from an ObjectInput stream (section 23.12). Blocks until some input is available; throws ObjectStreamException on end-of-stream.
`writeObject`	Serializes objects to an ObjectOutput stream (section 23.12).
`skip(n)`	Skips at most n bytes (from InputStreams) or n characters (from Readers). If $n>0$, blocks until some input is available; if $n<0$, throws IllegalArgumentException; returns 0 on end-of-stream.
`flush`	Writes any buffered data to the underlying stream, then flushes that stream. The effect is to make sure that all data have actually been written to the file system or the network.
`close`	Flushes and closes the stream, then flushes and closes all underlying streams. Further operations on the stream, except `close`, will throw IOException. Buffered writers and output streams should be explicitly closed or flushed to make sure that all data have been written; otherwise output data may be lost, even in case of normal program termination.

23.3   Imports, Exceptions, Thread Safety

A program using the input and output classes may contain the import declaration

```
import java.io.*;
```

Most input and output operations can throw an exception of class IOException or one of its subclasses, all of which are checked exceptions (chapter 15). Hence a method doing input or output must either do so in a `try-catch` block (section 12.6.6) or must contain the declaration `throws IOException` (section 9.8).

The standard implementation of input-output is thread-safe: multiple concurrent threads (chapter 16) can safely read from or write to the same stream without corrupting it. However, the Java class library documentation is not explicit on this point, so probably one should avoid using the same stream from multiple threads, or explicitly synchronize on the stream.

Example 141 Input-Output: Twelve Examples in One

This example illustrates input and output with human-readable text files; input and output of primitive values with binary files; input and output of arrays and objects with binary files; input and output of primitive values with random access binary files; input and output using strings and string builders; output to standard output and standard error; and input from standard input.

These brief examples do not use buffering, but input and output from files, sockets, and so on should use buffering for efficiency (section 23.13).

```java
// Write numbers and words on file "f.txt" in human-readable form:
PrintWriter pwr = new PrintWriter(new FileWriter("f.txt"));
pwr.print(4711); pwr.print(' '); pwr.print("cool"); pwr.close();
// Read numbers and words from human-readable text file "f.txt":
StreamTokenizer stok = new StreamTokenizer(new FileReader("f.txt"));
int tok = stok.nextToken();
while (tok != StreamTokenizer.TT_EOF)
  { System.out.println(stok.sval); tok = stok.nextToken(); }
// Write primitive values to a binary file "p.dat":
DataOutputStream dos = new DataOutputStream(new FileOutputStream("p.dat"));
dos.writeInt(4711); dos.writeChar(' '); dos.writeUTF("cool"); dos.close();
// Read primitive values from binary file "p.dat":
DataInputStream dis = new DataInputStream(new FileInputStream("p.dat"));
System.out.println(dis.readInt()+"|"+dis.readChar()+"|"+ dis.readUTF());
// Write an object or array to binary file "o.dat":
ObjectOutputStream oos = new ObjectOutputStream(new FileOutputStream("o.dat"));
oos.writeObject(new int[] { 2, 3, 5, 7, 11 }); oos.close();
// Read objects or arrays from binary file "o.dat":
ObjectInputStream ois = new ObjectInputStream(new FileInputStream("o.dat"));
int[] ia = (int[])(ois.readObject());
System.out.println(ia[0]+","+ia[1]+","+ia[2]+","+ia[3]+","+ia[4]);
// Read and write parts of file "raf.dat" in arbitrary order:
RandomAccessFile raf = new RandomAccessFile("raf.dat", "rw");
raf.writeDouble(3.1415); raf.writeInt(42);
raf.seek(0); System.out.println(raf.readDouble() + " " + raf.readInt());
// Read from a String s as if it were a text file:
Reader r = new StringReader("abc");
System.out.println("abc: " + (char)r.read() + (char)r.read() + (char)r.read());
// Write to a StringBuilder as if it were a text file:
Writer sw = new StringWriter();
sw.write('d'); sw.write('e'); sw.write('f');
System.out.println(sw.toString());
// Write characters to standard output and standard error:
System.out.println("std output"); System.err.println("std error");
// Read characters from standard input (the keyboard):
System.out.print("Type some characters and press Enter: ");
BufferedReader bisr = new BufferedReader(new InputStreamReader(System.in));
String response = bisr.readLine();
System.out.println("You typed: '" + response + "'");
// Read a byte from standard input (the keyboard):
System.out.print("Type one character and press Enter: ");
byte b = (byte)System.in.read();
System.out.println("First byte of your input is: " + b);
```

23.4 Sequential Character Input: Readers

The abstract class Reader and its subclasses (all having names ending in Reader) are used for character-oriented sequential input. In addition to the classes shown here, see BufferedReader (section 23.13) and LineNumber-Reader (example 146). The Reader class has the following methods:

- `void close()` flushes and closes the stream and any underlying stream. Any subsequent operation, except `close`, will throw IOException.
- `void mark(int limt)` marks the current input position, permitting at least `limt` characters to be read before calling `reset`.
- `boolean markSupported()` is `true` if the reader supports setting of marks and resetting to latest mark.
- `int read()` reads one character (with code 0...65535) and returns it. Blocks until input is available, or end-of-stream is reached (and then returns −1), or an error occurs (and then throws IOException).
- `int read(char[] b)` reads at most `b.length` characters into `b` and returns the number of characters read. Blocks until at least one character is available unless `b.length` is 0. Returns −1 on end-of-stream.
- `int read(char[] b, int i, int n)` works like the preceding, but reads into `b[i..(i+n-1)]`. Throws IndexOutOfBoundsException if `i<0` or `n<0` or `i+n>b.length`.
- `boolean ready()` returns `true` if the next `read` or `skip` will not block.
- `void reset()` resets the stream to the position of the latest call to `mark`.
- `int skip(int n)` skips at most n characters and returns the number of characters skipped; returns 0 on end-of-stream.

23.4.1 Reading Characters from a Byte Stream: InputStreamReader and Character Encoding

An InputStreamReader is a reader (a character input stream) that reads from a byte input stream, assembling bytes into characters using a character encoding. It performs buffered input from the underlying stream. An InputStreamReader has the same methods as a Reader (section 23.4), and also this constructor and method:

- `InputStreamReader(InputStream is)` creates an InputStreamReader from `is`, using the platform's standard character encoding to convert bytes to characters.
- `InputStreamReader(InputStream is, String enc)` creates an InputStreamReader that uses character encoding `enc`, for instance `"US-ASCII"` or `"ISO-8859-1"` (Latin1) or `"UTF-8"` or `"UTF-16"` or `"UTF-16BE"` (big-endian 16-bit) or `"UTF-16LE"` (little-endian 16-bit) or `"Cp1252"` (MS Windows).
- `String getEncoding()` returns the canonical name of the character encoding used by this reader.

23.4.2 Sequential Character Input from a File: FileReader

A FileReader is a buffered character input stream associated with a (sequential) file, and equivalent to an InputStreamReader created from a FileInputStream. It has the same methods as InputStreamReader, and these constructors:

- `FileReader(String name)` creates a character input stream associated with the named file. Throws FileNotFoundException if the file does not exist, is a directory, or cannot be opened for other reasons.
- `FileReader(File file)` creates a character input stream from the given file in the file system.
- `FileReader(FileDescriptor fd)` creates a character input stream from the file descriptor.

23.5   Sequential Character Output: Writers

The abstract class Writer and its subclasses (all having names ending in Writer) are used for character-oriented sequential output. They have the following methods:

- void close() flushes and closes the stream.
- void flush() actually writes data to the underlying stream or file, and then flushes that.
- void write(char[] b) writes the contents of character array b.
- void write(char[] b, int i, int n) writes n characters from b starting at position i; throws IndexOutOfBoundsException if i<0 or n<0 or i+n>b.length.
- void write(int c) writes a single character, namely, the two low-order bytes of c.
- void write(String s) writes string s.
- void write(String s, int i, int n) writes n characters from s starting at position i; throws StringIndexOutOfBoundsException if i<0 or n<0 or i+n>s.length.

23.5.1   Writing Characters to a Byte Stream: OutputStreamWriter

An OutputStreamWriter is a writer (character output stream) that writes to a byte output stream, converting characters to bytes using a character encoding. It performs buffered output to the underlying stream. An OutputStreamWriter has the same methods as a Writer (section 23.5), and in addition these constructors and method:

- OutputStreamWriter(OutputStream os) creates an OutputStreamWriter that writes to stream os using the platform's default character encoding.
- OutputStreamWriter(OutputStream os, String enc) creates an OutputStreamWriter that writes to stream os using the character encoding specified by enc; see section 23.4.1 for some valid enc values and example 151 for a typical use.
- String getEncoding() returns the canonical name of the character encoding used by this writer.

23.5.2   Sequential Character Output to a File: FileWriter

A FileWriter is a buffered character output stream associated with a (sequential) file, equivalent to an OutputStreamWriter created from a FileOutputStream. It has the same methods as OutputStreamWriter, and these constructors:

- FileWriter(String name) creates a character output stream and associates it with the named file in the file system. If the file exists, then it truncates the file; otherwise it tries to create a new empty file. Throws FileNotFoundException if the named file is a directory or cannot be opened or created for some other reason.
- FileWriter(String file, boolean append) works like the previous method, but if append is true, it does not truncate the file: instead output will be appended to the existing file contents.
- FileWriter(File file) works like the previous method, but creates the writer from file.
- FileWriter(FileDescriptor fd) works like the previous method, but creates the writer from fd.

23.6   Printing Primitive Data to a Character Stream: PrintWriter

The class PrintWriter is used to output primitive data to text files in human-readable form. Unlike the methods of other Writers, those of PrintWriter never throw IOException but set the error status. The PrintWriter class has all the methods of Writer, and in addition these constructors and methods:

- `PrintWriter(OutputStream os)` creates a PrintWriter that prints to stream os, without autoflush.
- `PrintWriter(OutputStream os, boolean flush)` creates a PrintWriter that prints to output stream os; if flush is true, then it flushes the writer after every call to println.
- `PrintWriter(Writer wr)` creates a PrintWriter that prints to the writer wr, without autoflush.
- `PrintWriter(Writer wr, boolean flush)` creates a PrintWriter that prints to the writer wr; if flush is true, then it flushes the writer after every call to println.
- `boolean checkError()` flushes the stream, then returns true if an error has ever occurred.
- `void print(boolean b)` prints the boolean b, that is, true or false.
- `void print(char c)` prints the character c.
- `void print(char[] cs)` prints the characters in cs.
- `void print(double d)` prints the double d.
- `void print(float f)` prints the float f.
- `void print(int i)` prints the integer i.
- `void print(long l)` prints the long integer l.
- `void print(Object o)` prints the object o using o.toString().
- `void print(String s)` prints the string s.
- `void println()` prints a single newline.
- `void println(e)` works like print(e) followed by println().

23.6.1   Standard Output: `System.out` and `System.err` Are PrintStreams

The standard output stream System.out and standard error stream System.err are PrintStreams. PrintStream is a subclass of OutputStream but in addition has methods print and println for character-based output, just as PrintWriter. These methods convert characters to bytes using the default encoding; to use another encoding enc, write to a PrintWriter created by `new PrintWriter(new OutputStreamWriter(System.out, enc))` as in example 151. Some possible values for enc are shown in section 23.4.1. The methods of a PrintStream never throw IOException, but set the error status; use checkError() to test the error status.

23.7   The Appendable Interface and the CharSequence Interface

The java.lang.Appendable interface (implemented by PrintStream, StringBuilder, StringBuffer and the Writer classes) describes three method overloads, all of which return a reference to the Appendable:

- `append(char c)` adds character c to the appendable.
- `append(CharSequence cseq)` adds all characters from cseq to the appendable.
- `append(CharSequence cseq, int i, int j)` adds characters i..j-1 from cseq.

The java.lang.CharSequence interface (implemented by String, StringBuilder and StringBuffer) describes methods charAt(int), length, subSequence(int,int), and toString; they behave as for String in section 7.

Example 142 Printing Numbers to a Text File
Simulate 1,000 rolls of a die and print the outcome to the text file dice.txt, 20 numbers to a line:

```
PrintWriter pw = new PrintWriter(new FileWriter("dice.txt"));
for (int i=1; i<=1000; i++) {
  int die = (int)(1 + 6 * Math.random());
  pw.print(die); pw.print(' ');
  if (i % 20 == 0) pw.println();
}
pw.println();
pw.close();                   // Without this, the output file may be empty
```

Example 143 Printing an HTML Table
This example generates a temperature conversion table in HTML. The Fahrenheit temperature f corresponds to the Celsius temperature $c = 5 \cdot (f - 32)/9$. The number of fractional digits is controlled by a formatting string. The HTML TABLE tag is used to control the alignment of numbers into columns.

  To print a conversion table in text format in a fixed-pitch font, replace the second pw.format call by pw.format("%10d%10.1f%n", f, c) and delete the other HTML-generating statements.

```
PrintWriter pw = new PrintWriter(new FileWriter("temperature.html"));
pw.println("<TABLE BORDER><TR><TH>Fahrenheit<TH>Celsius</TR>");
for (int f=100; f<=400; f+=10) {
  double c = 5 * (f - 32.0) / 9;
  pw.format("<TR ALIGN=RIGHT><TD>%d<TD>%.1f%n", f, c);
}
pw.println("</TABLE>");
pw.close();                   // Without this, the output file may be empty
```

Example 144 Using the Appendable Interface
The Expr abstract syntax for simple expressions below has a method output that writes the expression in text form to the given Appendable. That way the expression can be formatted to a StringBuilder, as a string, to standard output and to other character streams far more efficiently than by using toString methods.

```
abstract class Expr {
  public abstract void output(Appendable sink) throws IOException;
}
class Cst extends Expr { ... }
class Add extends Expr {
  Expr e1, e2;
  public Add(Expr e1, Expr e2) { this.e1 = e1; this.e2 = e2; }
  public void output(Appendable sink) throws IOException {
    sink.append('('); e1.output(sink); sink.append('+');
    e2.output(sink); sink.append(')');
} }
...
Expr expr = ...;
expr.output(System.out); System.out.println();      // To standard output
StringBuilder sb = new StringBuilder();              // To StringBuilder
expr.output(sb);
String s = sb.toString();                            // To String
Writer wr = new FileWriter("expr.txt");
expr.output(wr); wr.append('\n');                    // To text file
```

23.8   Reading Primitive Data from a Character Stream: StreamTokenizer

Reading words and numbers from a character stream is more complicated than printing them, so there is no text input counterpart to PrintWriter. Instead create a StreamTokenizer from a Reader.

A StreamTokenizer collects characters into tokens. Characters are classified as white space (separating tokens), number characters (making up a number token), word characters (making up a word token), quote characters (delimiting a string token), end-line comment characters (initiating a comment extending to end-of-line), or ordinary characters (none of the preceding).

A StreamTokenizer can be created and configured using this constructor and these methods and fields:

- `StreamTokenizer(Reader r)` creates a StreamTokenizer that reads from stream `r`.
- `void commentChar(int ch)` tells the tokenizer that `ch` is an end-line comment character.
- `void eolIsSignificant(boolean b)` tells the tokenizer to consider newline as a separate token of type `TT_EOL`, not as white space, if `b` is `true`.
- `void ordinaryChars(int c1, int c2)` tells the tokenizer that any character in the range `c1..c2` (inclusive) is an ordinary character: a single-character token, with `ttype` set to the character code.
- `void parseNumbers()` tells the tokenizer to recognize number tokens. A number token is a "word" beginning with a decimal digit (`0..9`) or a decimal point (`.`) or a minus sign (`-`), and consisting only of these three kinds of characters, so numbers in scientific notation `6.02e23` are not recognized. A number token has type `TT_NUMBER`.
- `void quoteChar(int ch)` tells the tokenizer that character `ch` is a string delimiter. When this character is encountered, `ttype` is set to `ch`, and `sval` is set to the string's contents: the characters strictly between `ch` and the next occurrence of `ch` or newline or end-of-stream.
- `void resetSyntax()` makes all characters ordinary; see `ordinaryChars`.
- `void whitespaceChars(int c1, int c2)` tells the tokenizer that all characters in the range `c1..c2` (inclusive) are white space also, that is, token separators.
- `void wordChars(int c1, int c2)` tells the tokenizer that all characters in the range `c1..c2` (inclusive) are word characters also.

Class StreamTokenizer has these methods and fields for reading values:

- `int lineno()` returns the current line number, counting from 1.
- `int nextToken()` reads the next (or first) token and returns its type.
- `double nval` is the number value of the current number token (when `ttype` is `TT_NUMBER`).
- `String sval` is the string value of the current word token (when `ttype` is `TT_WORD`), or the string body of the current string token (when `ttype` is a quote character).
- `int ttype` is the type of the current token. The type may be `StreamTokenizer.TT_NUMBER`, indicating a number, or `StreamTokenizer.TT_WORD`, indicating a word, or `StreamTokenizer.TT_EOL`, indicating a newline, or `StreamTokenizer.TT_EOF`, indicating end-of-stream (no more tokens), or a quote character, indicating a string (in quotes), or any other character, indicating that character as a token by itself.

While a StreamTokenizer is useful for reading fairly simple text files, more structured text files should be read using a proper lexer and parser (see common textbooks for compiler courses) or special-purpose libraries (e.g., for XML files or XML streams).

Example 145 Reading Numbers from a Text File

A StreamTokenizer stok is created from a buffered file reader and told to recognize number tokens. Tokens are read until end-of-stream, and the number tokens are added together, whereas non-number tokens are printed to standard output. The buffering of input is important: it makes the program more than 20 times faster.

```
static void sumfile(String filename) throws IOException {
  Reader r = new BufferedReader(new FileReader(filename));
  StreamTokenizer stok = new StreamTokenizer(r);
  stok.parseNumbers();
  double sum = 0;
  stok.nextToken();
  while (stok.ttype != StreamTokenizer.TT_EOF) {
    if (stok.ttype == StreamTokenizer.TT_NUMBER)
      sum += stok.nval;
    else
      System.out.println("Nonnumber: " + stok.sval);
    stok.nextToken();
  }
  System.out.println("The file sum is " + sum);
}
```

Example 146 Reading Numbers from a Text File, Line by Line

A StreamTokenizer stok is created from a LineNumberReader and told to recognize number tokens and new-lines. Tokens are read until end-of-stream, and the sum of the number tokens is computed line by line. The line number is set to count from 1 (default is 0). Class LineNumberReader is a subclass of BufferedReader and therefore is already buffered. Using a LineNumberReader is somewhat redundant, since StreamTokenizer itself provides a lineno() method.

```
static void sumlines(String filename) throws IOException {
  LineNumberReader lnr = new LineNumberReader(new FileReader(filename));
  lnr.setLineNumber(1);
  StreamTokenizer stok = new StreamTokenizer(lnr);
  stok.parseNumbers();
  stok.eolIsSignificant(true);
  stok.nextToken();
  while (stok.ttype != StreamTokenizer.TT_EOF) {
    int lineno = lnr.getLineNumber();
    double sum = 0;
    while (stok.ttype != StreamTokenizer.TT_EOL) {
      if (stok.ttype == StreamTokenizer.TT_NUMBER)
        sum += stok.nval;
      stok.nextToken();
    }
    System.out.println("Sum of line " + lineno + " is " + sum);
    stok.nextToken();
  }
}
```

23.9   Sequential Byte Input: InputStream

The abstract class InputStream and its subclasses (all of whose names end in InputStream) are used for byte-oriented sequential input. They have the following methods:

- `int available()` returns the number of bytes that can be read or skipped without blocking.
- `void close()` closes the stream.
- `void mark(int limt)` marks the current input position, permitting at least `limt` bytes to be read before calling `reset`.
- `boolean markSupported()` returns `true` if the stream supports `mark` and `reset`.
- `int read()` reads one byte ($0 \ldots 255$) and returns it, blocking until input is available; returns -1 on end-of-stream.
- `int read(byte[] b)` reads at most `b.length` bytes into `b`, blocking until at least one byte is available; then returns the number of bytes actually read. Returns -1 on end-of-stream.
- `int read(byte[] b, int i, int n)` reads at most `n` bytes into `b` at position `i`, blocking until at least one byte is available, and returns the number of bytes actually read. Returns -1 on end-of-stream. Throws IndexOutOfBoundsException if `i<0` or `n<0` or `i+n>b.length`.
- `void reset()` repositions the stream to the position at which the `mark` method was last called.
- `long skip(long n)` skips at most `n` bytes, blocking until a byte is available, and returns the number of bytes actually skipped. Returns 0 if end-of-stream is reached before input is available.

The standard input `System.in` is an InputStream; to read characters from it, create an InputStreamReader using `new InputStreamReader(System.in)`; see example 141.

23.9.1   Sequential Byte Input from File: FileInputStream

A FileInputStream is an InputStream that reads sequentially from an existing file on the file system. It has the same methods as InputStream (section 23.9), and these constructors and additional method:

- `FileInputStream(String name)` creates a byte input stream and associates it with file `name` in the file system. Throws FileNotFoundException if the file does not exist, is a directory, or cannot be opened.
- `FileInputStream(File file)` works like the preceding, but associates the stream with `file`.
- `FileInputStream(FileDescriptor fd)` works like the preceding, but associates the stream with `fd`.
- `FileDescriptor getFD()` returns the file descriptor associated with this stream.

23.9.2   Sequential Binary Input of Primitive Data: DataInputStream

Class DataInputStream provides methods for machine-independent sequential binary input of Java primitive types such as `int` and `double`. The class implements the DataInput interface (section 23.11) and in addition provides this constructor and static method:

- `DataInputStream(InputStream is)` creates a DataInputStream that reads from stream `is`.
- `static String readUTF(DataInput di)` reads a Java UTF-8 encoded string from stream `di`.

Class DataInputStream also has a `readLine` method which is deprecated. To read lines of text from a Data-InputStream, create an InputStreamReader (section 23.4.1) from it instead.

23.10   Sequential Byte Output: OutputStream

The abstract class OutputStream and its subclasses (all of whose names end in OutputStream) are used for byte-oriented sequential output. It has the following methods:

- void close() closes the output stream.
- void flush() flushes the output stream and forces any buffered output bytes to be written to the underlying stream or file, then flushes that.
- void write(byte[] b) writes b.length bytes from b to the output stream.
- void write(byte[] b, int i, int n) writes n bytes from b starting at offset i to the output stream. Throws IndexOutOfBoundsException if i<0 or n<0 or i+n>b.length.
- void write(int b) writes the byte b (0...255) to the output stream.

23.10.1   Sequential Byte Output to a File: FileOutputStream

A FileOutputStream is an OutputStream that writes sequentially to a file on the file system. It has the same methods as OutputStream (section 23.10) and these constructors and additional method:

- FileOutputStream(String name) creates a byte output stream and associates it with the named file in the file system. If the file exists, then it is truncated; otherwise, an attempt is made to create the file. Throws FileNotFoundException if the file is a directory or cannot be opened or created for some other reason.
- FileOutputStream(String name, boolean append) works like the preceding, but if append is true, then does not truncate the file: instead output will be appended to any existing file contents.
- FileOutputStream(File file) works like the preceding but associates the stream with file.
- FileOutputStream(FileDescriptor fd) works like the preceding but associates the stream with fd.
- FileDescriptor getFD() returns the file descriptor associated with this stream.

23.10.2   Sequential Binary Output of Primitive Data: DataOutputStream

Class DataOutputStream provides methods for machine-independent sequential binary output of Java primitive types such as int and double. The class implements the DataOutput interface (section 23.11) and provides this constructor and method:

- DataOutputStream(OutputStream os) creates a DataOutputStream that writes to the stream os.
- int size() returns the number of bytes written to this DataOutputStream.

23.11 Binary Input-Output of Primitive Data: DataInput and DataOutput

The interfaces DataInput (implemented by DataInputStream, ObjectInputStream, and RandomAccessFile) and DataOutput (implemented by DataOutputStream, ObjectOutputStream and RandomAccessFile) describe operations for byte-oriented input and output of values of primitive type, such as `boolean`, `int`, and `double`. Thus DataInput's method `readInt()` is suitable for reading integers written using DataOutput's method `writeInt(int)`. The data format is platform-independent.

The DataInput interface describes the following methods. The read and skip methods block until the required number of bytes have become available, and throw EOFException if end-of-stream is reached first.

- `boolean readBoolean()` reads one input byte and returns `true` if non-zero, `false` otherwise.
- `byte readByte()` reads one input byte and returns a byte in range $-128\ldots127$.
- `char readChar()` reads two bytes and returns a character in range $0\ldots65535$.
- `double readDouble()` reads eight bytes and returns a double.
- `float readFloat()` reads four bytes and returns a float.
- `void readFully(byte[] b)` reads exactly `b.length` bytes into buffer b.
- `void readFully(byte[] b, int i, int n)` reads exactly n bytes into `b[i..(i+n-1)]`.
- `int readInt()` reads four bytes and returns an integer.
- `String readLine()` reads a line of one-byte characters in the range $0\ldots255$ (not Unicode).
- `long readLong()` reads eight bytes and returns a long integer.
- `short readShort()` reads two bytes and returns a short integer $-32768\ldots32676$.
- `int readUnsignedByte()` reads one byte and returns an integer in the range $0\ldots255$.
- `int readUnsignedShort()` reads two bytes and returns an integer in the range $0\ldots65535$.
- `String readUTF()` reads a string encoded using the Java modified UTF-8 format.
- `int skipBytes(int n)` skips exactly n bytes of data and returns n.

The DataOutput interface describes the following methods. Note that `writeInt(i)` writes four bytes representing the Java integer i, whereas `write(i)` writes one byte containing the low-order eight bits of i.

- `void write(byte[] b)` writes all the bytes from array b.
- `void write(byte[] b, int i, int n)` writes n bytes from array `b[i..(i+n-1)]`.
- `void write(int v)` writes the eight low-order bits of byte v.
- `void writeBoolean(boolean v)` writes one byte: 1 if v is `true`, otherwise 0.
- `void writeByte(int v)` writes the low-order byte (eight low-order bits) of integer v.
- `void writeBytes(String s)` writes the low-order byte of each character in s (not Unicode).
- `void writeChar(int v)` writes two bytes (high-order, low-order) representing v.
- `void writeChars(String s)` writes the string s, two bytes per character.
- `void writeDouble(double v)` writes eight bytes representing v.
- `void writeFloat(float v)` writes four bytes representing v.
- `void writeInt(int v)` writes four bytes representing v.
- `void writeLong(long v)` writes eight bytes representing v.
- `void writeShort(int v)` writes two bytes representing v.
- `void writeUTF(String s)` writes two bytes of (byte) length information, followed by the Java modified UTF-8 representation of every character in the string s.

Example 147 Binary Input and Output of Primitive Data

Method `writedata` demonstrates all ways to write primitive data to a DataOutput stream (a stream of class DataInputStream or RandomAccessFile). Similarly, method `readdata` demonstrates all ways to read primitive values from a DataInput stream (a stream of class DataOutputStream or RandomAccessFile). The methods complement each other, so after writing a stream with `writedata`, one can read it using `readdata`.

```java
public static void main(String[] args) throws IOException {
  DataOutputStream daos = new DataOutputStream(new FileOutputStream("tmp1.dat"));
  writedata(daos); daos.close();
  DataInputStream dais = new DataInputStream(new FileInputStream("tmp1.dat"));
  readdata(dais);
  RandomAccessFile raf = new RandomAccessFile("tmp2.dat", "rw");
  writedata(raf); raf.seek(0); readdata(raf);
}
static void writedata(DataOutput out) throws IOException {
  out.writeBoolean(true);                            // Write 1 byte
  out.writeByte(120);                                // Write 1 byte
  out.writeBytes("foo");                             // Write 3 bytes
  out.writeBytes("fo");                              // Write 2 bytes
  out.writeChar('A');                                // Write 2 bytes
  out.writeChars("foo");                             // Write 6 bytes
  out.writeDouble(300.1);                            // Write 8 bytes
  out.writeFloat(300.2F);                            // Write 4 bytes
  out.writeInt(1234);                                // Write 4 bytes
  out.writeLong(12345L);                             // Write 8 bytes
  out.writeShort(32000);                             // Write 2 bytes
  out.writeUTF("foo");                               // Write 2 + 3 bytes
  out.writeUTF("Rhône");                             // Write 2 + 6 bytes
  out.writeByte(-1);                                 // Write 1 byte
  out.writeShort(-1);                                // Write 2 bytes
}
static void readdata(DataInput in) throws IOException {
  byte[] buf1 = new byte[3];
  System.out.print(        in.readBoolean());        // Read 1 byte
  System.out.print(" " + in.readByte());             // Read 1 byte
  in.readFully(buf1);                                // Read 3 bytes
  in.readFully(buf1, 0, 2);                          // Read 2 bytes
  System.out.print(" " + in.readChar());             // Read 2 bytes
  System.out.print(" " + in.readChar()+in.readChar()+in.readChar());
  System.out.print(" " + in.readDouble());           // Read 8 bytes
  System.out.print(" " + in.readFloat());            // Read 4 bytes
  System.out.print(" " + in.readInt());              // Read 4 bytes
  System.out.print(" " + in.readLong());             // Read 8 bytes
  System.out.print(" " + in.readShort());            // Read 2 bytes
  System.out.print(" " + in.readUTF());              // Read 2 + 3 bytes
  System.out.print(" " + in.readUTF());              // Read 2 + 6 bytes
  System.out.print(" " + in.readUnsignedByte());     // Read 1 byte
  System.out.print(" " + in.readUnsignedShort());    // Read 2 bytes
  System.out.println();
}
```

23.12   Serialization of Objects: ObjectInput and ObjectOutput

The interfaces ObjectInput (implemented by ObjectInputStream) and ObjectOutput (implemented by ObjectOutputStream) describe operations for byte-oriented input and output of values of reference type, that is, objects and arrays. This is also called *serialization* or *marshalling*.

An object or array can be serialized (converted to a sequence of bytes) if its class and all classes on which the object or array depends have been declared to implement the interface Serializable. The Serializable interface does not declare any methods; it only serves to show that the class admits serialization.

Serialization of an object o writes the object's non-static (instance) fields, except those declared `transient`, to the stream. When the object is deserialized, a `transient` field gets the default value for its type (`false` or 0 or 0.0 or `null`). Class fields (`static` fields) are not serialized.

Serialization to an ObjectOutputStream preserves sharing among the objects written to it, and more generally, preserves the form of the object reference graph. For instance, if object o1 and o2 both refer to a common object c (so o1.c == o2.c), and o1 and o2 are serialized to ObjectOutputStream oos, then object c is serialized only once to oos. When o1 and o2 are restored again from oos, then c is restored also, exactly once, so o1.c == o2.c holds as before. If o1 and o2 are serialized to two different ObjectOutputStreams, then restoration of o1 and o2 will produce two distinct copies of c, so o1.c != o2.c. Thus sharing among objects is not preserved across multiple ObjectOutputStreams.

The interface ObjectInput (implemented by ObjectInputStream) has all the methods specified by DataInput, and the following additional ones. The methods `available()`, `close()`, `read(byte[])`, `read(byte[], int, int)`, and `skip(int)` behave like those of class InputStream (section 23.9).

- `int available()` returns the number of bytes that can be read or skipped without blocking.
- `void close()` closes the stream, as in InputStream.
- `int read()` reads one byte, as in InputStream.
- `int read(byte[] b)` reads bytes into b, as in InputStream.
- `int read(byte[] b, int i, int n)` reads into b[i..(i+n-1)], as in InputStream.
- `Object readObject()` reads, deserializes, and returns an object, which must have been previously serialized. Throws ClassNotFoundException if the declaration (class file) for an object that is being deserialized cannot be found. Throws ObjectStreamException or one of its subclasses if no object can be read from the stream, e.g., if end-of-stream is encountered before the object is complete.
- `long skip(long n)` skips n bytes, as in InputStream.

The interface ObjectOutput (implemented by ObjectOutputStream) has all the methods of interface DataOutput (section 23.11) and the following additional one.

- `void writeObject(Object obj)` writes the object using serialization. All classes being serialized must implement the Serializable interface; otherwise NotSerializableException is thrown.

Interface Externalizable is a subinterface of Serializable that can be implemented by classes that need full control over the serialization and deserialization of their objects.

Example 148 Serialization to the Same ObjectOutputStream Preserves Sharing
Objects o1 and o2 refer to a shared object c of class SC. We serialize o1 and o2 to the same file using a single
ObjectOutputStream, so we get a single copy of the shared object. When we deserialize the objects and bind
them to variables o1i and o2i, we also get a single copy of the shared SC object:

```
class SC implements Serializable { int ci; }
class SO implements Serializable {
  int i; SC c;
  SO(int i, SC c) { this.i = i; this.c = c; }
  void cprint() { System.out.print("i" + i + "c" + c.ci + " "); }
}
...
File f = new File("objects.dat");
// Create the objects and write them to file.
SC c = new SC();
SO o1 = new SO(1, c), o2 = new SO(2, c);
o1.c.ci = 3; o2.c.ci = 4;                    // Update the shared c twice
o1.cprint(); o2.cprint();                    // Prints: i1c4 i2c4
OutputStream os = new FileOutputStream(f);
ObjectOutputStream oos = new ObjectOutputStream(os);
oos.writeObject(o1); oos.writeObject(o2); oos.close();
// Read the objects from file.
InputStream is = new FileInputStream(f);
ObjectInputStream ois = new ObjectInputStream(is);
SO o1i = (SO)(ois.readObject()), o2i = (SO)(ois.readObject());
o1i.cprint(); o2i.cprint();                  // Prints: i1c4 i2c4
o1i.c.ci = 5; o2i.c.ci = 6;                  // Update the shared c twice
o1i.cprint(); o2i.cprint();                  // Prints: i1c6 i2c6
```

Example 149 Serialization to Distinct ObjectOutputStreams Does Not Preserve Sharing
If we serialize the objects o1 and o2 from example 148 to the same file using two different ObjectOutput-
Streams, each object stream will write a copy of the shared object. When we deserialize the objects, we get
two copies of the previously shared SC object:

```
// Create the objects (as in above example) and write them to file.
ObjectOutputStream oos1 = new ObjectOutputStream(os);
oos1.writeObject(o1); oos1.flush();
ObjectOutputStream oos2 = new ObjectOutputStream(os);
oos2.writeObject(o2); oos2.close();
// Read the objects from file, non-shared c.
InputStream is = new FileInputStream(f);
ObjectInputStream ois1 = new ObjectInputStream(is);
SO o1i = (SO)(ois1.readObject());
ObjectInputStream ois2 = new ObjectInputStream(is);
SO o2i = (SO)(ois2.readObject());
o1i.cprint(); o2i.cprint();                  // Prints: i1c4 i2c4
o1i.c.ci = 5; o2i.c.ci = 6;                  // Update two different c's
o1i.cprint(); o2i.cprint();                  // Prints: i1c5 i2c6
```

23.13 Buffered Input and Output

Writing one byte or character at a time to a file or network connection is very inefficient. It is better to collect the bytes or characters in a buffer, and then write the whole buffer in one operation. The same holds for reading from a file or network connection. However, buffering will not speed up input from and output to byte arrays, character arrays, strings, or string buffers.

To buffer a plain input stream is, create a BufferedInputStream from is and read from that stream instead; and similarly for output streams, readers, and writers.

The operation flush() can be used on a buffered stream to request that the output actually gets written to the underlying stream. A buffered stream should be properly closed by a call to close() to ensure that all data written to the buffer are eventually written to the underlying stream.

Class BufferedReader has all the methods of class Reader (section 23.4) and these constructors and method:

- BufferedReader(Reader rd) creates a buffered reader that reads from rd.

- BufferedReader(Reader rd, int sz) creates a buffered reader with buffer of size sz. It throws IllegalArgumentException if sz <= 0.

- String readLine() reads a line of text. A line is terminated by line feed ("\n") or carriage return ("\r") or carriage return and line feed ("\r\n"). Returns the line without any line termination characters; returns null at end-of-stream.

Class BufferedWriter has all the methods of Writer (section 23.5) and also these constructors and method:

- BufferedWriter(Writer wr) creates a buffered writer that writes to stream wr.

- BufferedWriter(Writer wr, int sz) creates a buffered writer with a buffer of size sz. It throws IllegalArgumentException if sz <= 0.

- void newLine() writes a line separator, such as "\n" or "\r\n", depending on the platform.

Class BufferedInputStream is a subclass of FilterInputStream. It has the same methods as InputStream (section 23.9) and these constructors:

- BufferedInputStream(InputStream is) creates a BufferedInputStream that reads from stream is.

- BufferedInputStream(InputStream is, int sz) creates a BufferedInputStream with buffer size sz; throws IllegalArgumentException if sz <= 0.

Class BufferedOutputStream is a subclass of FilterOutputStream. It has the same methods as OutputStream (section 23.10) and these constructors:

- BufferedOutputStream(OutputStream os) creates a BufferedOutputStream that writes to stream os.

- BufferedOutputStream(OutputStream os, int sz) creates a BufferedOutputStream with a buffer of size sz; throws IllegalArgumentException if sz <= 0.

Example 150 Output Buffering

Buffering may speed up writes to a FileOutputStream by a large factor. Buffering the writes to a FileWriter has less effect, because a FileWriter is an OutputStreamWriter, which buffers the bytes converted from written characters before writing them to an underlying FileOutputStream. In one experiment, buffering made writes to a FileOutputStream 18 times faster and writes to a FileWriter only two or three times faster.

```
public static void main(String[] args) throws IOException {
  OutputStream os1 = new FileOutputStream("tmp1.dat");
  writeints("Unbuffered: ", 1000000, os1);
  OutputStream os2 = new BufferedOutputStream(new FileOutputStream("tmp2.dat"));
  writeints("Buffered:   ", 1000000, os2);
  Writer wr1 = new FileWriter("tmp1.dat");
  writeints("Unbuffered: ", 1000000, wr1);
  Writer wr2 = new BufferedWriter(new FileWriter("tmp2.dat"));
  writeints("Buffered:   ", 1000000, wr2);
}
static void writeints(String msg, int count, OutputStream os) throws IOException {
  Timer t = new Timer();
  for (int i=0; i<count; i++)
    os.write(i & 255);
  os.close();
  System.out.println(msg + t.check());
}
static void writeints(String msg, int count, Writer os) throws IOException {
  Timer t = new Timer();
  for (int i=0; i<count; i++)
    os.write(i & 255);
  os.close();
  System.out.println(msg + t.check());
}
```

For efficiency, one should usually wrap buffered streams around file streams and socket streams as follows:

Replace	By
new FileInputStream(e)	new BufferedInputStream(new FileInputStream(e))
new FileOutputStream(e)	new BufferedOutputStream(new FileOutputStream(e))
new FileWriter(e)	new BufferedWriter(new FileWriter(e))
new FileReader(e)	new BufferedReader(new FileReader(e))

Example 151 Specifying a Particular Output Encoding

To print to a file or standard output with character encoding enc, create an OutputStreamWriter (from a File-OutputStream or System.out) with that encoding and then use it to create a PrintWriter. Some legal encodings are listed in section 23.4.1. In UTF-8, the character 's' is encoded in one byte, as in US-ASCII or ISO-8859-1, but the character 'ü' (latin small letter u with diaeresis) is encoded as two bytes: $195 = (192 + 252 \text{ div } 64)$ and $188 = (128 + 252 \text{ mod } 64)$, because the Unicode number of 'ü' is 252. All numbers here are in decimal.

```
String s = "El Niño, süß, Ærøskøbing å, éclair, §2";
String enc = "UTF-8";          // 8-bit Unicode encoding
OutputStreamWriter osw = new OutputStreamWriter(System.out, enc);
PrintWriter pw = new PrintWriter(osw);
pw.println(s);
```

23.14   Random Access Files: RandomAccessFile

Class RandomAccessFile is used for input from and output to so-called *random access files*. The data in a random access file can be accessed in any order, in contrast to streams, which can be read and written only sequentially from the beginning. Thus a random access file is similar to an extensible byte array stored on the file system. A random access file has an associated file pointer, which determines where the next read or write operation will begin. Setting the file pointer permits random access to all parts of the file (albeit thousands or millions times more slowly than to a byte array stored in memory). The file pointer is an offset from the beginning of the file; the first byte in the file has offset 0, the last byte in a file `raf` has offset `raf.length()-1`. The method call `seek(pos)` sets the file pointer to point at byte number `pos`.

Class RandomAccessFile implements the DataInput and DataOutput interfaces (section 23.11) and has the following constructors and additional methods. The methods `read()`, `read(byte[])`, and `read(byte[], int, int)` behave as in InputStream (section 23.9); in particular, they return −1 on end-of-file, and block until at least one byte of input is available. The methods `readt()`, where `t` is a type, behave as in DataInput (section 23.11); in particular, they throw EOFException on end-of-file.

- `RandomAccessFile(String name, String mode)` creates a new random access file stream and associates it with a file of the given name on the file system. Initially the file pointer is at offset 0. Throws IOException if the name indicates a directory. The `mode` must be `"r"` for read-only, or `"rw"` for read-write; otherwise IllegalArgumentException is thrown. If the file does not exist on the file system, and the mode is `"r"`, then FileNotFoundException is thrown, but if the mode is `"rw"`, then a new empty file is created if possible. If the mode is `"r"`, any call to the `write` methods will throw IOException.

- `RandomAccessFile(File file, String mode)` works like the preceding, but associates the random access file stream with `file`.

- `void close()` closes the file stream.

- `FileDescriptor getFD()` returns the file descriptor associated with the stream.

- `long getFilePointer()` returns the current value of the file pointer.

- `long length()` returns the length of the file in bytes.

- `int read()` reads one byte, as in InputStream.

- `int read(byte[] b)` reads into array b, as in InputStream.

- `int read(byte[] b, int i, int n)` reads at most n bytes into b, as in InputStream.

- `void seek(long pos)` sets the file pointer to byte number pos. Throws IOException if `pos<0`. The file pointer may be set beyond end-of-file; a subsequent write will then extend the file's length.

- `void setLength(long newlen)` sets the length of the file by truncating or extending it (at the end); in the case of extension, the content of the extension is undefined.

Example 152 Organizing a String Array File for Random Access
This example shows a way to implement random access to large numbers of texts, such as millions of cached Web pages or millions of DNA sequences. We define a string array file to have three parts: (1) a sequence of Strings, each of which is in Java modified UTF-8 format; (2) a sequence of long integers, representing the start offsets of the strings; and (3) an integer, which is the number of strings in the file. (Note that Java limits the length of each UTF-8-encoded string; using a slightly more complicated representation in the file, we could lift this restriction.)

By putting the number of strings and the string offset table at the end of the file rather than at the beginning, we do not need to know the number of strings or the length of each string before writing the file. The strings can be written to the file incrementally, and the only structure we need to keep in memory is the table (ArrayList) of string lengths.

Method writeStrings takes as argument a file name and a string generator in the form of an Iterable<String>. The first (enhanced) for statement creates an Iterator<String> from the iterable, and writes the strings produced by the iterator to the file while storing the offsets in the offset table. The second (enhanced) for statement writes the offsets to the file subsequently.

```
static void writeStrings(String filename, Iterable<String> strGenerator)
  throws IOException {
  RandomAccessFile raf = new RandomAccessFile(filename, "rw");
  raf.setLength(0);                             // truncate the file
  ArrayList<Long> offsettable = new ArrayList<Long>();
  for (String s : strGenerator) {
    offsettable.add(raf.getFilePointer());      // store string offset
    raf.writeUTF(s);                            // write string
  }
  for (long offset : offsettable)
    raf.writeLong(offset);
  raf.writeInt(offsettable.size());             // write string count
  raf.close();
}
```

Example 153 Random Access Reads from a String Array File
The method call readOneString(f, i) reads string number i from a string array file f (example 152) in three stages, using three calls to seek. First, it reads the offset table length N from the last 4 bytes of the file. Second, since an int takes 4 bytes and a long takes 8 bytes (section 5.1), the string offset table must begin at position length()-4-8*N, and so the offset si of string number i can be read from position length()-4-8*N+8*i. Third, the string itself is read from offset si.

```
static String readOneString(String filename, int i) throws IOException {
  final int INTSIZE = 4, LONGSIZE = 8;
  RandomAccessFile raf = new RandomAccessFile(filename, "r");
  raf.seek(raf.length() - INTSIZE);
  int N = raf.readInt();
  raf.seek(raf.length() - INTSIZE - LONGSIZE * N + LONGSIZE * i);
  long si = raf.readLong();
  raf.seek(si);
  String s = raf.readUTF();
  raf.close();
  return s;
}
```

23.15   Files, Directories, and File Descriptors

23.15.1   Path Names in a File System: Class File

An object of class File represents a path name, that is, a directory/file path in the file system. The path name may denote a directory, a data file, or nothing at all (if there is no file or directory of that name). Even if the path name denotes a file or directory, a given program may lack the permission to read or write that file or directory. These are a few of the constructors and methods in class File:

- File(String pname) creates a path name corresponding to the string pname.
- boolean exists() returns true if a file or directory denoted by this path name exists.
- String getName() returns this path name as a string.
- boolean isDirectory() tests whether the file denoted by this path name is a directory.
- boolean isFile() tests whether the file denoted by this path name is a normal file.
- long length() returns the length of the file in bytes, or 0 if the file does not exist.
- File[] listFiles() returns the files and directories in the directory denoted by the path name; returns null on error or if the path name does not denote a directory.
- boolean mkdir() creates the directory named by this path name.

23.15.2   File System Objects: Class FileDescriptor

An object of class FileDescriptor is a file descriptor, an internal representation of an active file system object, such as an open file or an open socket. A file descriptor may be obtained from a FileInputStream (section 23.9) or FileOutputStream (section 23.10). The class has this method:

- void sync() requests that all system buffers are synchronized with the underlying physical devices; blocks until this has been done. Throws SyncFailedException if it cannot be done.

The class has static fields in, out, and err, which are the file descriptors associated with the standard input (System.in), standard output (System.out), and standard error (System.err) streams.

23.16   Thread Communication: PipedInputStream and PipedOutputStream

Threads (chapter 16) execute concurrently and may communicate asynchronously using internal pipes. A *pipe* is a pair of a PipedInputStream and a PipedOutputStream, or a pair of a PipedReader and a PipedWriter. By contrast, communication with other processes or with remote computers uses InputStreams and OutputStreams, possibly obtained from operating system sockets, briefly described in section 23.17.

To create a pipe, create one end of it by outpipe = new PipedOutputStream(), then use that to create and connect the other end by inpipe = new PipedInputStream(outpipe). Either end may be created first. A pipe end can be connected only once.

A producer thread writes to a PipedOutputStream (or PipedWriter), and a consumer thread reads from a PipedInputStream (or PipedReader) associated with the PipedOutputStream (or PipedWriter). If the producer thread is fast and the pipe fills up, then the next write operation blocks until there is room for data in the pipe. If the consumer thread is fast and there are no available data in the pipe, then the next read operation blocks until data become available. When either the consumer or the producer dies, and one end of the pipe is destroyed, the next write (or read) at the other end of the pipe throws an IOException.

Example 154 Reading and Printing a Directory Hierarchy

The call showDir(0, pathname) will print the path name, and if the path name exists and is a directory, then showDir recursively prints all its subdirectories and files. Because indent is increased for every recursive call, the layout reflects the directory structure.

```
static void showDir(int indent, File file) throws IOException {
  for (int i=0; i<indent; i++)
    System.out.print('-');
  System.out.println(file.getName());
  if (file.isDirectory()) {
    File[] files = file.listFiles();
    for (int i=0; i<files.length; i++)
      showDir(indent+4, files[i]);
  }
}
```

Example 155 Internal Pipes Between Threads

The producer thread writes the infinite sequence of prime numbers $2, 3, 5, 7, 11, 13, \ldots$ to a PipedOutputStream, while the consumer (the main thread) reads from a PipedInputStream connected to the PipedOutputStream. Actually, the producer writes to a DataInputStream built on top of the PipedOutputStream, and the consumer reads from a DataInputStream built on top of the PipedInputStream, because we want to send integers, not only bytes, through the pipe.

```
PipedOutputStream outpipe = new PipedOutputStream();
PipedInputStream inpipe = new PipedInputStream(outpipe);
final DataOutputStream outds = new DataOutputStream(outpipe);
DataInputStream inds = new DataInputStream(inpipe);
// This thread outputs primes to outds -> outpipe -> inpipe -> inds:
class Producer extends Thread {
  public void run() {
    try {
      outds.writeInt(2);
      for (int p=3; true; p+=2) {
        int q=3;
        while (q*q <= p && p%q != 0)
          q+=2;
        if (q*q > p)
          { outds.writeInt(p); System.out.print("."); }
      }
    } catch (IOException e) { System.out.println("<terminated>: " + e); }
  }
}

new Producer().start();
for (;;) {                                    // Forever
  for (int n=0; n<10; n++)                     //   output 10 primes
    System.out.print(inds.readInt() + " ");    //   and
  System.in.read();                            //   wait for Enter
}
```

23.17   Socket Communication

Whereas a pair of Java threads can communicate through a local pipe (e.g., PipedInputStream), a pair of distinct processes may communicate through *sockets*. The processes may be on the same machine, or on different machines connected by a network.

Sockets are often used in client/server architectures, where the server process creates a *server socket* that listens for connections from clients. When a client connects to the server socket, a fresh socket is created on the server side and is connected to the socket that the client used when connecting to the server. The socket connection is used for bidirectional communication between client and server; both ends can obtain an input stream and an output stream from the socket.

Here are a constructor and some methods from the ServerSocket class in package `java.net`:

- `ServerSocket(int port)` creates a server socket on the given `port`.
- `Socket accept()` listens for a connection, blocking until a connection is made. Creates and returns a new Socket when a connection is made. If a timeout is set, the call to `accept` throws InterruptedIOException when the timeout expires.
- `void close()` closes the server socket.
- `void setSoTimeout(int tmo)` sets the timeout so that a call to `accept` will time out after `tmo` milliseconds, if positive. Disables timeout if `tmo` is zero; timeout is disabled by default.

Here are a constructor and some methods from the Socket class in package `java.net`:

- `Socket(String host, int port)` creates a client socket and connects to a given `port` on the given `host`. The `host` may be a name (`"localhost"`) or an IP address (`"127.0.0.1"`).
- `void close()` closes the socket.
- `InetAddress getInetAddress()` returns the address to which this socket is connected, as an object of class `java.net.InetAddress`; methods `getHostName()` and `getHostAddress()` can be used to convert this address to a string.
- `InputStream getInputStream()` returns the input stream associated with this socket.
- `OutputStream getOutputStream()` returns the output stream associated with this socket.
- `void setSoTimeout(int tmo)` sets the timeout so that a call to `read` on the input stream obtained from this socket will time out after `tmo` milliseconds, if positive. If `tmo` is zero, then timeout is disabled (the default). If a timeout is set, a call to `read` throws InterruptedIOException when the timeout expires.

The Socket and ServerSocket classes are declared in the Java class library package `java.net`. The Java class library documentation [3] provides more information about sockets and server sockets.

Example 156 Socket Communication Between Processes

This example program runs as a server process or as a client process, depending on the first command line argument. The server and client may run on the same machine, or on different machines communicating via a network. Several clients may connect to the same server. The server creates a server socket that accepts connections on port 2357. When a client connects, a new client socket is created and an integer is received on that socket. If the integer is a prime, the server replies `true` on the same socket, otherwise `false`.

Each client process asks the server about the primality of the numbers 1 through 999 and prints those that are primes.

It is rather inefficient for the client to create a new socket for every request to the server, but it suffices for this example. Also, buffering the input and output streams may speed up socket communication (section 23.13).

```java
import java.io.*;
import java.net.*;

class SocketTest {
  final static int PORT = 2357;

  public static void main(String[] args) throws IOException {
    boolean server = args.length == 1 && args[0].equals("server");
    boolean client = args.length == 2 && args[0].equals("client");
    if (server) {                  // Server: accept questions about primality
      ServerSocket serversock = new ServerSocket(PORT);
      for (;;) {
        Socket sock = serversock.accept();
        DataInputStream dis  = new DataInputStream(sock.getInputStream());
        DataOutputStream dos = new DataOutputStream(sock.getOutputStream());
        int query = dis.readInt();
        dos.writeBoolean(isprime(query));
        dis.close(); dos.close();
      }
    } else if (client) {           // Client: ask questions about primality
      for (int i=1; i<1000; i++) {
        Socket sock = new Socket(args[1], PORT);
        DataOutputStream dos = new DataOutputStream(sock.getOutputStream());
        DataInputStream dis = new DataInputStream(sock.getInputStream());
        dos.writeInt(i);
        if (dis.readBoolean())
          System.out.print(i + " ");
        dos.close(); dis.close();
      }
    } else { ... }                 // Neither server nor client
  }

  static boolean isprime(int p) { ... return true if p is prime ... }
}
```

24   Reflection

Reflection permits a running program to inspect and manipulate the classes, interfaces, methods and fields of the program itself. For every non-generic type t in a running Java program, there is an object ot of class java.lang.Class that represents type t. From ot one can get representations of the members (fields, methods and nested types) of type t, as well as other information. Using reflection, one can create objects and arrays, call methods, and get and set the value of fields, but one cannot directly create new types, nor add new methods to existing types. Third-party libraries such as BCEL [9] support the creation of new types.

Reflection provides powerful dynamic adaptability, but implies that the usual checks (of argument types in a method call, for instance) cannot be performed at compile-time. Instead they must be performed at run-time, and this takes time, so reflection is slow, and may fail, so exceptions may be thrown; see section 24.4.

24.1   Reflective Use of Types: The Class<T> Class

If t is a type, then the expression t.class of type Class<t> evaluates to the unique object ot that represents type t at run-time. The type t may be a class C or interface I or an array type such as int[] or an enum type or annotation type or a primitive type such as int or the pseudo-type void. It cannot be a generic type G<T> or a type instance such as G<Integer>; instead one must use the raw type G, as in G.class.

When o has reference type and is non-null, the expression o.getClass() has raw type Class, and evaluates to the unique object that represents the run-time type of o. Class Class<t> has the following methods:

- static Class Class.forName(String name) returns the Class object representing the class called name, loading the class if not already loaded.
- int getModifiers() returns the modifiers of the class; see example 163.
- t newInstance() returns a new object of the class, created as if by a call to an argumentless constructor.
- boolean isInstance(Object o) returns true if o is non-null and could be assigned to a variable of type t, where t is the type represented by the Class object; otherwise false.
- t cast(Object o) of type t returns o if o could be assigned to a variable of the type t represented by the Class object; otherwise throws ClassCastException. In particular, succeeds if o is null.

Thus isInstance and cast are dynamic versions of instanceof and type cast (sections 11.8 and 11.11).

In addition, class Class<t> has methods to get the fields, methods, constructors, and nested types of type t, shown below. The methods on the left return only public members, including inherited ones, whereas the methods on the right return only members declared in the class, not inherited ones:

	Public Members (Including Inherited Ones)	Declared Members (Including Non-Public Ones)
Single	Field getField(name)	Field getDeclaredField(name)
	Method getMethod(name, parTy)	Method getDeclaredMethod(name, parTy)
	Constructor<t> getConstructor(parTy)	Constructor<t> getDeclaredConstructor(parTy)
All	Field[] getFields()	Field[] getDeclaredFields()
	Method[] getMethods()	Method[] getDeclaredMethods()
	Constructor[] getConstructors()	Constructor[] getDeclaredConstructors()
	Class[] getClasses()	Class[] getDeclaredClasses()

A field is identified by its name (a String), a method is identified by its name and parameter types parTy (an array Class[] or a parameter array Class...), and a constructor is identified by its parameter types parTy. The types Field, Method and Constructor are explained in sections 24.2 and 24.3.

Example 157 Listing Public Methods and Declared Methods

Class C1 declares two public and one private method, and its subclass C2 declares a public and a private method. The getMethods call gets C2's inherited methods m1(), m1(int), its public method m3, and those inherited from Object (equals, hashCode, ...). The getDeclaredMethods call gets C2's declared methods m3 and m4.

```java
import java.lang.reflect.*;
class C1 {
  public int f1;
  protected int f2;
  public C1() { }
  public C1(int f1) { this.f1 = f1; }
  public void m1()      { System.out.println("C1.m1()"); }
  public void m1(int i) { System.out.println("C1.m1(int)"); }
  private void m2()     { System.out.println("C1.m2()"); }
}
class C2 extends C1 {
  public void m3()  { System.out.println("C2.m3()"); }
  private void m4() { System.out.println("C2.m4()"); }
}
class Reflection1 {
  public static void main(String[] args) {
    Class<C2> c2o = C2.class;
    Method[] mop = c2o.getMethods();          // Gets m1() m1(int) m3() ...
    Method[] mod = c2o.getDeclaredMethods();  // Gets m3() m4()
} }
```

Example 158 The Unique Class Object of a Class; and the Run-Time Class of an Object

Consider the classes C1 and C2 from example 157. The class object for a given class is unique, so the class object c2o obtained from class C2 is identical to the class object c2o2 obtained from an instance o2 of C2 using method getClass. Also, note that the getClass method returns the *run-time class* of an object, so o11 and o12 have different getClass values although they have the same compile-time type C1.

```java
Class<C2> c2o = C2.class;
C2 o2 = new C2();
Class c2o2 = o2.getClass();          // c2o == c2o2
C1 o11 = new C1(), o12 = o2;         // o11.getClass() != o12.getClass()
if (o11.getClass() != o12.getClass()) ...
```

Example 159 Reflective Object Creation, Instance Tests, and Casts

Still using the classes from example 157, we can create an object o21 of class C2 from the class object c2o that represents C2, test whether the existing object o12 is an instance of C2 (it is), and test whether the existing object o11 is an instance of C2 (it is not). Also, a cast of o12 to C2 succeeds and the expression has type C2 because c2o has compile-time type Class<C2>, but a cast of string "foo" to C2 fails by throwing a ClassCastException.

```java
Class<C2> c2o = C2.class;
C2 o2 = new C2();
C1 o11 = new C1(), o12 = o2;
C2 o21 = c2o.newInstance();    // well-typed: c2o has type Class<C2>
if (c2o.isInstance(o12)) ...   // true
if (c2o.isInstance(o11)) ...   // false
C2 c22 = c2o.cast(o12);        // succeeds at run-time: o12 can be cast to C2
C2 c23 = c2o.cast("foo");      // fails at run-time
```

24.2   Reflection: The Field Class

An object of class Field from package `java.lang.reflect` represents a static or non-static field in a class or interface. It supports the following operations:

- `Object get(Object o)` returns the value of the field (in object o if an instance field).
- `int getModifiers()` returns the modifiers of the field; see example 163.
- `String getName()` returns the name of the field.
- `Class getType()` returns the type of the field.
- `Class getDeclaringClass()` returns the class containing the field's declaration.
- `void set(Object o, Object v)` sets the value of the field to v (in object o if an instance field).

24.3   Reflection: The Method Class and the Constructor<T> Class

An object of class Method from package `java.lang.reflect` represents a static or non-static method, and supports the following operations:

- `String getName()` returns the name of the method.
- `Class[] getParameterTypes()` returns the formal parameter types of the method.
- `Class[] getExceptionTypes()` returns the exception classes listed in the method's `throws` clause.
- `Class getDeclaringClass()` returns the class containing the method's declaration.
- `int getModifiers()` returns the modifiers of the method; see example 163.
- `Class getReturnType()` returns the method's declared return type.
- `Object invoke(Object o, Object... args)` invokes the method on object o, passing the arguments args, and returns the result of the method, or `null` if the return type is `void`. If the method is static then o is ignored and may be `null`; if the method is non-static then o must be non-`null` and becomes the current object reference `this` in the method invocation.
- `boolean isVarArgs()` returns true if the method has variable arity (section 9.9).

An object of class Constructor<t> from package `java.lang.reflect` represents a constructor from class t, and permits creation of objects of that class. Class Constructor<t> supports the same operations as class Method, except for `getReturnType`, and has this additional operation:

- `newInstance(Object... args)` returns a new object instance of the constructor's class. The expression has type t when the constructor object has type Constructor<t>, and it has type Object when the constructor object has (raw) type Constructor. Note that `newInstance` has variable arity.

24.4   Exceptions Thrown When Using Reflection

Operations on a Class, Field, Method or Constructor may throw IllegalAccessException (field, method or constructor is inaccessible); or IllegalArgumentException (wrong type of object o when using an instance field or method; or wrong argument type when getting or setting a field; or wrong argument type when invoking a method); or InstantiationException (the called constructor belongs to an abstract class); or InvocationTarget-Exception (an invoked method threw an exception); or NoSuchFieldException; or NoSuchMethodException; or NullPointerException (the given object reference o is `null` when using an instance field or method).

Example 160 Reflective Access to a Field
The Field object f1o represents the (inherited) field f1 in class C2 from example 157. The value of the field can be set and accessed reflectively. An attempt to get field f2 from c2o will fail with NoSuchFieldException.

```
Class<C2> c2o = C2.class;
Field f1o = c2o.getField("f1");
C2 o2 = new C2();
f1o.set(o2, 117);                                    // Sets o2.f1 to 117
System.out.format("Value of o2.f1 = %d%n", f1o.get(o2)); // Gets o2.f1
Class<C1> c1o = C1.class;
Field f21 = c1o.getDeclaredField("f2");
```

Example 161 Reflective Retrieval and Invocation of a Method
Variables m1o and m1io represent methods m1() and m1(int) from class C1 in example 157. When invoking the instance methods a C1 object is needed; this may be an object of a subclass such as C2. Note how parameter types (int) are specified and how arguments (117) are passed using parameter arrays (section 9.9).

```
Class<C1> c1o = C1.class;
Method m1o = c1o.getMethod("m1"),              // Gets C1.m1()
       m1io = c1o.getMethod("m1", int.class);  // Gets C1.m1(int)
C2 o2 = new C2();
m1o.invoke(o2);                                // Call o2.m1()
m1io.invoke(o2, 117);                          // Call o2.m1(117)
```

Example 162 Reflective Creation of an Object
The compile-time type of cc1o is Constructor<C1> so the compile-time type of cc1o.newInstance(42) is C1, but that of cco.newInstance(42) is Object. The class C1 is from example 157.

```
Class<C1> c1o = C1.class;
Constructor<C1> cc1o = c1o.getConstructor(int.class);  // Gets C1(int)
Constructor cco = cc1o;
C1 c11 = cc1o.newInstance(42);                 // Compile-time type C1
Object c12 = cco.newInstance(56);              // Compile-time type Object
```

Example 163 Reflective Inspection of Modifiers: static, private, ...
The result of a getModifiers method can be inspected using static methods or bitwise 'and' (&) with symbolic constants from class Modifier. This example prints the private methods from the Method array mod:

```
for (Method m : mod)
  if (Modifier.isPrivate(m.getModifiers()))
    System.out.println(m);
```

Modifier or Declaration	Test	Symbolic Constant
abstract	Modifier.isAbstract(mods)	Modifier.ABSTRACT
final	Modifier.isFinal(mods)	Modifier.FINAL
interface	Modifier.isInterface(mods)	Modifier.INTERFACE
private	Modifier.isPrivate(mods)	Modifier.PRIVATE
protected	Modifier.isProtected(mods)	Modifier.PROTECTED
public	Modifier.isPublic(mods)	Modifier.PUBLIC
static	Modifier.isStatic(mods)	Modifier.STATIC
synchronized	Modifier.isSynchronized(mods)	Modifier.SYNCHRONIZED
transient	Modifier.isTransient(mods)	Modifier.TRANSIENT

25   Metadata Annotations (Java 5.0)

Annotations are used to attach meta-data to a *target*, where a target may be a constructor declaration, a field declaration, a local variable declaration, a method declaration, a package declaration, a parameter declaration, a type declaration (class, interface, enum type), or the declaration of another annotation type.

An annotation of type Anno is attached to its target by writing @Anno(f1=e1, ..., fn=en) before the target declaration. The type of an annotation argument ei can be a simple type or Object or String or Class or an enum type or an annotation type or an array of one of these types. Each expression ei must be compile-time constant or a one-dimensional array {...} of compile-time constants. A target can have only one annotation of a given annotation type; but an annotation may contain an array of other annotations. An annotation that takes no arguments can be written @Anno instead of @Anno(). An annotation that takes a single argument called value can be used as @Anno("Ulrik") instead of @Anno(value="Ulrik").

The declaration of an annotation type @Anno has this form:

```
interface-modifiers @interface Anno {
  annotation-members
}
```

Each *annotation-member* has one of these three forms, where an *annotation-member-expression* is a compile-time constant:

```
type f();
type f() default annotation-member-expression;
final type f = constant;
```

Several meta-annotations may be used when declaring an annotation type. The @TARGET({...}) meta-annotation specifies the legal targets for an annotation type; the default is any target:

@TARGET Value	Legal Targets
ANNOTATION_TYPE	Annotation type declarations
CONSTRUCTOR	Constructor declarations
FIELD	Field declarations or enum value declarations
LOCAL_VARIABLE	Local variable declarations
METHOD	Method declarations
PACKAGE	Package declarations
PARAMETER	Parameter declarations in method or constructor
TYPE	Class or interface or enum type declarations

The @RETENTION(...) meta-annotation specifies the retention policy for an annotation type:

Value	Meaning
STATIC	The annotation is discarded by the compiler and will not be stored in the class file
CLASS	The annotation is stored in the class-file (default) but unavailable at run-time
RUNTIME	The annotation is available for reflective inspection at run-time

Annotations with retention policy RUNTIME can be accessed using reflection (section 24) at run-time. Methods getAnnotations and getDeclaredAnnotations on classes Class, Field, Method and Constructor return the annotations of the given target in an array of type Annotation[].

If an annotation that has meta-annotation @INHERITED is used on a class declaration, then the subclasses of this class will inherit the annotation.

Example 164 Declaring and Using a Custom Annotation Type

An Author annotation is a custom annotation that holds an author name, a month (of enum type Month from example 88), a diet, and a weekly workload. Its legal targets are classes and methods. Author annotations are retained until run-time, so they can be inspected using reflection as shown in the main method. Note the use of static import (section 18) to avoid prefixing TYPE and METHOD with their declaring enum type, which is java.lang.annotation.ElementType. An Authors annotation is simply an array of Author annotations.

```java
import java.lang.annotation.*;                     // Annotation
import static java.lang.annotation.ElementType.*;  // @Target arguments
import static java.lang.annotation.RetentionPolicy.*;  // @Retention arguments
import java.lang.reflect.*;                        // Method

@Target({TYPE, METHOD})     // Attribute can be used on types and methods only
@Retention(RUNTIME)         // Attribute values are kept until run-time
@interface Author {
  public final int oneHour = 60 * 60 * 1000;
  public String name();
  public Month month();
  public String[] diet() default { "Coffee", "Cola", "Mars bars" };
  public int weeklyWork() default 56 * oneHour;
}

@Retention(RUNTIME)         // Attribute values are kept until run-time
@interface Authors {
  public Author[] value();
}

class TestAnnotations {
  @Author(name="Peter", month=Month.Nov, diet={ "Dr. Pepper" })
  public void myMethod1() { }

  @Author(name="Jens", month=Month.Jul)
  public void myMethod2() { }

  @Authors({@Author(name="Ulrik", month=Month.Jul),
            @Author(name="Andrzej", month=Month.Aug, diet = { "Tea" })})
  public void myMethod3() { }

  public static void main(String[] args) {
    Class ty = TestAnnotations.class;
    for (Method mif : ty.getMethods()) {
      if (mif.getName().startsWith("myMethod")) {
        System.out.println("\nGetting the annotations of " + mif.getName());
        // This finds only annotations with RUNTIME retention
        Annotation[] annos = mif.getDeclaredAnnotations();
        System.out.println("The annotations are:");
        for (Annotation anno : annos)
          System.out.println(anno);
      }
    }
  }
}
```

26   What Is New in Java 5.0

Many new features have been added to the Java programming language in version 5.0, notably:

- A new reserved name, enum; see section 2.

- Automatic boxing and unboxing of primitive type values, for instance from int to Integer and vice versa; see section 5.4.

- Extensive support for formatting of numbers and dates as strings; see section 7.1.

- Variable-arity methods and constructors; see section 9.9.

- Enhanced for statement for convenient iteration over collections, dictionaries and other objects that are iterable, that is, provide an iterator; see sections 12.5.2 and 22.7.

- Typesafe enum types; see section 14.

- Static imports; see section 18 and examples 164 and 165.

- Class StringBuilder provides a faster unsynchronized replacement for StringBuffer; see section 20.

- Generic types and methods: classes, interfaces and methods can have type parameters; section 21.

- The collection classes have much better compile-time type safety due to generic types; see section 22.

- Metadata annotations; see section 25.

Most of these features are found also in the C# programming language, although some of them have been added only recently, in C# version 2.0, as shown by this table:

	Java		C#	
Feature	1.4	5.0	1.1	2.0
Looping over iterators	−	+	+	+
Defining iterators (C# yield statement)	−	−	−	+
Enum types	−	+	+	+
Autoboxing simple values	−	+	+	+
Nullable value types	−	−	−	+
Generic types and methods	−	+	−	+
Run-time type parameter information	−	−	−	+
Wildcard types in generic instances	−	+	−	−
Anonymous methods	−	−	−	+
Annotations (metadata, attributes)	−	+	+	+

Example 165 New Features in Java 5.0
This example illustrates the new features mentioned opposite, except for annotations, which are illustrated by
example 164. Note the use of log instead of Math.log and out.println instead of System.out.println
due to the static import clauses.

```java
import static java.lang.System.*;               // For field out
import static java.lang.Math.*;                  // For methods log, exp
import java.util.*;                               // For class LinkedList<T>

class TestNewFeatures {
  public static void main(String[] args) {
    double giga = exp(30.0 * log(2.0));
    out.println("2^30 = " + giga);                // 2^30 = 1.073741823999999E9
    out.format("2^30 = %12.2f\n", giga);          // 2^30 = 1073741824.00
    String res = concat("Cop", "en", "hagen");
    out.format("result = %s\n", res);             // result = Copenhagen
    Direction dir = Direction.North;
    dir = dir.turnLeft();
    out.println(dir);                             // West
    List<Double> list = new ArrayList<Double>();  // Generic collection type
    list.add(7.2); list.add(22.4); list.add(-9.2);// Boxing to Double
    for (double d : list)                         // Unboxing to double
      out.format("%+7.1f\n", d);                  // Fixed-width formatting
  }

  static String concat(String... ss) {           // Variable-arity method
    StringBuilder sb = new StringBuilder();       // StringBuilder
    for (String s : ss)                           // ss is a String array
      sb.append(s);
    return sb.toString();
  }

  enum Direction {
    East, North, West, South;                     // Enum values

    public Direction turnLeft() {                 // Member method
      switch (this) {                             // Switch on enum value
      case East:  return Direction.North;
      case North: return Direction.West;
      case West:  return Direction.South;
      case South: return Direction.East;
      default: throw new RuntimeException("Impossible");
      }
    }
  }
}
```

References

[1] The authoritative reference on the Java programming language (version 1.4 and earlier) is J. Gosling, B. Joy, G. Steele, and G. Bracha, *Java Language Specification*, 2nd ed. (Boston: Addison Wesley, 2000). Browse or download in HTML (573 KB) or PDF at <http://java.sun.com/docs/books/jls/>.

The *Java Language Specification* is currently being updated; its third edition will describe Java 5.0.

[2] An introduction to all aspects of Java programming is K. Arnold, J. Gosling, and D. Holmes, *The Java Programming Language*, 3rd ed. (Boston: Addison Wesley, 2000).

[3] The Java class libraries (or Java Core API) are described in two volumes of *The Java Class Libraries, Second Edition* (Boston: Addison Wesley, 1997/98). Volume 1, by P. Chan, R. Lee, and D. Kramer, covers java.io, java.lang, java.math, java.net, java.text, and java.util. Volume 2, by P. Chan and R. Lee, covers java.applet, java.awt, and java.beans. Also available is P. Chan, R.Lee, and D. Kramer, *The Java Class Libraries: 1.2 Supplement* (Boston: Addison Wesley, 1999).

The class library documentation can be browsed at <http://java.sun.com/docs/> or downloaded as a zip-file (43.5 MB) from the same place.

[4] An excellent guide to good programming in Java is *Effective Java Programming Language Guide* (Addison-Wesley 2001) by Joshua Bloch.

[5] A compact guide to Java code style is *The Elements of Java Style* (Cambridge: Cambridge University Press, 2000) by A. Vermeulen *et al.*

[6] The Java Tutorials from Sun Microsystem provide a wealth of general and specialized information on Java, for free. See <http://java.sun.com/docs/books/tutorial/>

[7] The Unicode character encoding (<http://www.unicode.org/>) corresponds to part of the Universal Character Set (UCS), which is international standard ISO 10646-1:2000. The UTF-8 is a variable-length encoding of UCS, in which seven-bit ASCII characters are encoded as themselves, described in Annex R of this standard.

[8] Floating-point arithmetic is described in the ANSI/IEEE Standard for Binary Floating-Point Arithmetic (IEEE Std 754-1985).

[9] Bytecode Engineering Library (BCEL). Home page at <http://jakarta.apache.org/bcel/>

Index